Praise for *Ladysitting*

"Rain dances nourishment
from the soil
Tears waltz love
from the heart
Sun dances a boogie
woogie while
Lorene Cary is *Ladysitting*
with her Grandmother
Question:
Who brings the beer?"
—Nikki Giovanni

"Cary's chronicle of this centenarian (+1) is written with candor, warmth, and love. The final chapters are critical reading for anyone with an aging loved one at the end of their life."
—Betsy Lerner, author of *The Bridge Ladies*

"[Cary] movingly portrays what it's like to care for a loved one." —Elizabeth Sile, *Real Simple*

"Open the cover of *Ladysitting*, and you're immediately yanked into a story with an ending you already know. . . . One of the more deftly-written, truthful accounts in this genre." —Terri Schlichenmeyer, *Washington Informer*

"A heartfelt, multifaceted story. . . . This reflective memoir steeped in love and forgiveness explores a devoted granddaughter's perceptions about her grandmother."
—*Shelf Awareness*

Ladysitting

Ladysitting

My Year with Nana at the End of Her Century

Lorene Cary

W. W. NORTON & COMPANY
Independent Publishers Since 1923

For information about permission to reproduce selections from this book,
write to Permissions, W. W. Norton & Company, Inc.,
500 Fifth Avenue, New York, NY 10110

For information about special discounts for bulk purchases, please contact
W. W. Norton Special Sales at specialsales@wwnorton.com or 800-233-4830

Manufacturing by Lake Book Manufacturing
Book design by Fearn Cutler de Vicq
Production manager: Lauren Abbate

Library of Congress Cataloging-in-Publication Data

Names: Cary, Lorene, author.
Title: Ladysitting : my year with nana at the end of her century / Lorene Cary.
Description: First edition. | New York : W. W. Norton & Company, [2019]
Identifiers: LCCN 2018053657 | ISBN 9780393635881 (hardcover)
Subjects: LCSH: Cary, Lorene. | Heart—Diseases—Patients—Biography. |
Caregivers—Biography. | Heart—Diseases—Patients—Family relationships.
| Grandparent and child—Biography.
Classification: LCC RC672 .C374 2019 | DDC 616.1/20092 [B]—dc23
LC record available at https://lccn.loc.gov/2018053657

ISBN 978-0-393-35823-0 pbk.

W. W. Norton & Company, Inc., 500 Fifth Avenue, New York, N.Y. 10110
www.wwnorton.com

W. W. Norton & Company Ltd., 15 Carlisle Street, London W1D 3BS

1 2 3 4 5 6 7 8 9 0

With love
to my own dear grandchildren:
Sam, Zach, Mica,
and Wrenna Ruby

Preface

Why was it that weekends at Nana Jackson's felt like a world apart? Maybe because, dressed in old ball gowns, I traveled with the sun patch across the floor of the suburban New Jersey neocolonial and soaked in more light and luxe than my parents' West Philadelphia apartment could ever offer. Delight and time, the wide-armed, fragrant mimosa to climb in summer, the fireplace to stoke in winter, and choices all the day long—"whatever your little heart desires."

Yes, yes, yes, I knew that I was being spoiled, that word that obsessed black grown-ups, and even kids. What could be worse than to be spoiled, ruined by indulgence, incapable of withstanding hardship as we had done and would do in future? We were brought up by hand as surely as Pip in *Great Expectations*, and much prouder of it than he. "You spoiled!" could get you a corrective beatdown. Fast. Besides, everybody needed to respect authority, learn limits, and above all, to know that older people valued you, that they loved your undeserving black behind enough to bring you back from wrong to right. I knew myself to be a wimp, a failure in the toughness category, which was why I went insane with terror at the sound of my mother coming for me, or my father reaching for the threatened, though seldom used, belt. If a kid down the street got a beating—and in our cheek-by-jowl row houses we heard each one—I'd be good for a month!

So, believe you me, as my mother would say before administering some firm guidance by hand, I knew good and well that my whole Nana deal was off-the-charts spoiling. Which was why, with peers, I kept it to myself. What happened in West Collingswood stayed in West Collingswood. Nana's weekend abundance did not feel unconditional, by any means. Our contract was that I would "occupy myself" while she got things done, and then she'd spoil me. But the time alone felt more like Sabbath, as if God visited me occasionally in those sun patches and let me curl up to Its presence.

Ecstatic! I learned in junior high school the word that retrofitted my memory of this meditative, out-of-time, out-of-body joy. It made a through line, connecting to when I was allowed to sit next to the beautiful Ward AME organist Ms. Selena, who bounced from the pew to the organ to the wooden box that got her up to where the choir could see her guiding them to breathe with one breath for us to share. Ecstatic connected to reading the ancient, but living, Bible with my great-grandfather from Barbados, born in the 1800s, who hailed from the other side of the family and the Caribbean. We read Samuel, so that if God called me, in the night, I'd know to say, "Speak, for your servant is listening." It connected to the Renaissance-era church prose we mumbled to confess to God our "transgressions against his Divine majesty." This ecstasy at Nana's and Pop-Pop's house, however, transcended transgressions in a childhood buzzing with anxiety about right and wrong and punishment.

One of my earliest memories with Nana, at her house, anchors the rest. I wanted a drink of water and went into the kitchen. Nana wasn't there, so I reached for a glass. They were small Libby juice glasses, diner-style, wavy and thin enough to feel beautiful against my palm. I forget whether I climbed up to reach the metal cabinet that opened with a ping or found the glass on the counter. Either way, I knew it was too high for me, and as I knew it, the tiny tumbler dropped from my hand onto the linoleum, where it crashed into sharp pieces.

Fear flooded me from scalp to gut. My mother had warned me to behave well on these weekends; she sent just-right outfits, perfectly laundered so I'd look like somebody cared; she instructed me how to make my hair twists last overnight, because Nana, with her straight hair, never could comb mine right, that is, fuzz-n-naps pulled back hard enough to straighten them. Above all, I was to do there what I had learned at home: to anticipate what was correct and do it before Nana had to ask.

Now, instead, I'd shattered one of the thousand glass hazards in this breakable house, with its bric-a-brac ceramic white faces and Chinese antique stuff everywhere—all things I was usually careful to look at, but never touch (except for the Chinese doll, which Nana would take out of the cabinet and let me hold in her presence). I'd get in trouble with Mommy for failing to be careful, and that would be bad, but I was used to it. What was worse, though, was that

I had broken the spell. I'd wrecked the charm of my magical place. Nana would be angry; and I would no longer be the trusted, free-range granddaughter, free to play records over and over and pick out tunes on the piano, and dress up, and roam freely to sing and draw and make up stories in the middle-class museum of her house and garden. I could hear her rushing down the carpeted steps. My gut wrenched with dread.

"Oh, honey," she asked when she stepped into the kitchen. "What happened?"

I knew I should admit the wrong and apologize. But how could I? The metal cabinet pressed cold against my back.

Nana looked back and forth, frowning, inspecting the scene like a diorama. She could see my original misjudgment, and, worse yet, the moment of willfulness when I knew better, but grabbed at the glass anyway. I was crying by now. That's what you get. I think I began apology blubber.

Nana took my right hand, turned it over, and then smiled. "I thought you had cut yourself," she said, clearly relieved. "We can always get another glass, but we can never get a new hand, can we?"

Sabbath returned, not a charm, but a peace we could choose. She never hit me.

And yet this person who provided kindness and delight to my sister and me was at the same time the woman of whom my father, her only child, once said, "She never loved me." As I moved into adulthood, Nana showed me more sides of herself, enough so that I understood, even as I grieved, why she and my father, who had seemed inseparable, had stopped speaking. What was love among them or us? Had it ever been real?

I'm writing to find out. I want not to forget, but to recall, how the end of my grandmother's life pulled into focus her hundred and one years on earth, the part we shared as well as the earlier life she brought with her into ours. I want to keep company with other families who have lived through and are living in the intense and demanding time of hospice. We underwent a mash-up of fear and mortality—she was dying, then living again, then dying—and memory and love.

Nana hinged angrily between ancestors coming close and descendants she was about to leave. Her story required me to learn more about the father she'd referred to with pride, but only glancingly, and it took me into the halls of Congress and the Jim Crow South he brought his family north to escape. It brought me closer to her son, my father, and drove me farther from him. Death up close and personal meant my husband and daughters, and my sister and her family, riding with Nana in family sidecars through her alt-universe of dreams and visions, and our own, through truth and lies, business and money, and communal and racial memory.

After she died, I felt stuck for years: I couldn't sweep up the odd bits of her business; I couldn't shake the sense that I had not done enough over that long, slow year and a half for her or for my other family members. I did not move easily through anger to acceptance. Nor could I do what I've done all my life: I couldn't write my way out. That was until Ash Wednesday three years ago. This narrative explores my struggle, like so many others', to find love again each time I lost it, because it is only love, as the Song of Solomon assures us, that is strong as death.

> Set me as a seal upon your heart,
>> as a seal upon your arm;
> for love is strong as death,
>> passion fierce as the grave.
> Its flashes are flashes of fire,
>> a raging flame.

> Many waters cannot quench love,
>> neither can floods drown it.
> If one offered for love
>> all the wealth of one's house,
>> it would be utterly scorned.

—Song of Solomon 8:6–7
New Revised Standard Version, 1989

Chapter 1

A month after Nana died, she started to come to me in dreams. She was sitting in her wheelchair, banging her fists on the padded arms, demanding that I get her back into her house in New Jersey. Weak and clouded over with cataracts she'd refused to have removed, her eyes nevertheless burned into me. "Get me into my house," she shouted. "I want to come back."

I knew that life force.

In her eighties Nana contracted pneumonia. She spent Mother's Day and then her birthday in Our Lady of Lourdes hospital under the neon halo of its namesake. When I brought a new pink nightgown to the hospital and she commanded in a whisper that I was to "save the nice box," I knew she'd make it.

In her mid-nineties Nana survived a car accident that plowed her head into the windshield as she drove home from work; a month later, as I drove her to her tiny South Philly real estate office, she asked whether I had any doubts about her buying a new car.

The summer she turned 100, Nana contracted a bladder

infection that started to take her down. It was midsummer 2007, and we were hosting a reunion of the descendants of the eleven Barbados Drayton siblings on my mother's side who came to the United States in the twentieth century. We held it at my husband's church in Philadelphia, with its protected greensward and sunny parish hall.

One cousin from Barbados stayed with us at the rectory. I'd cooked and refrigerated three kinds of meat stew she liked to eat for breakfast on the kitchen porch where she could watch the birds. Hummingbirds came to the feeder; they were my husband's favorite, but my cousin developed a special fondness for "those large brown birds that pull worms from the ground after rain. What are they?"

When we told her, she shouted: "Robin? Robin redbreas'?" Were these indeed the "robin redbreasts" of her postcolonial, but still thoroughly English, grammar-school readers? Oh, dear, dear robin redbreasts that live in the Northern Hemisphere and in the English romantic imagination imported for Caribbean schoolchildren in poetry and worship. My cousin called to them lovingly across the lawn.

I made a mental note to tell Nana the robin redbreast anecdote that evening. I took her these stories along with food treats, often with lightbulbs, when I visited her three, four, five, six times a week, at her house, just across the Walt Whitman Bridge from Philadelphia. The visits were as necessary as food and water. We kept up an ongoing conversation, disagreeing gently at predictable intersections, about human nature and meaning and hope.

This was the summer the last Harry Potter was published, and my sister Carole, who buys the best presents,

ordered our younger daughter Zoë one of those early copies. The Barbadian cousin met Zoë's excitement with disap-
proval. Weren't these books about witchcraft? Didn't that fly
in the face of the teachings of our Lord and Savior?

No doubt I would have added that to the story I'd tell
Nana. Maybe Nana would laugh outright. I'd wonder aloud,
in ways that would bore her, about faith that gives hope vs.
faith that guarantees.

Toward the end of the reunion, though, I was tired,
so I decided to ring Nana to tell her I wouldn't come that
night; instead I'd see her the next morning. But Nana did
not answer. I rang several times, the same number she'd had
since I can remember, the second phone number I ever memorized, with an exchange that began with UL for Ulysses.
I did not even bother to ring her cell phone, even though
she'd used it to call me a few times when she had a problem
with the landline. I found my sister Carole and asked her to
come with me on the half-hour drive to Nana's house in West
Collingswood, which would take us only twenty minutes that
night. Our older daughter Laura, who'd just graduated college, said she'd come, too. At eleven, Laura had been with
us when the undertakers came after the death of Pop-Pop,
Nana's husband. We stayed with Nana as they carried Pop's
body down the stairs and out the door in a body bag that
looked like corduroy. To this day the two emergency drives
over the bridge meld together in her mind.

On the way I rang Nana's doctor. By now, he was in his
nineties, with a geriatric schedule, no answering service, and
a home phone he might or might not answer, with or without
hearing aid. If he was asleep, there'd be a long grappling with

the receiver followed only by a startled near-shout: "Hello!": no name, no "Dr. ——, here," nothing to distinguish him from a wrong number to the nursing home. Even back when his office had regular hours and normal doctorly protocols, my sister would sometimes ask me whether I thought he was a quack. True enough, Nana liked her medical and financial professionals controllable.

On a recent phone call, Carole had asked me whether he was still licensed. After training at Columbia's Graduate School of Journalism and working as a reporter, followed by marriage, a successful corporate career, and two children, Carole turned to lengthy training as a flight instructor and finally professional pilot. She handles gargantuan volumes of factual material. Had she lived here, my sister the pilot would have checked to see whether the man responsible for Nana's care still had a valid New Jersey license to practice medicine. I was ashamed to say that I didn't know. Nana would not have wanted to know. Nana didn't care.

"She's strong, very strong, so it probably won't kill 'er," the doctor said of her current infection. "But on the other hand, it might."

Pause. Beat. Silence.

"So your suggestion? If she were your family member, what would you do?" I pushed.

"Call an ambulance and get her to the hospital."

We stepped into the house we all knew as well as we knew our own. To me it smelled as it always did: dry, a little dusty, with kitchen and fireplace scents as low background notes.

The relatively new smell of urine from her next-to-the-bed bucket hit us on the landing, just past the blue-and-white ceramic Chinese garden stool where I used to sit when no one was looking. Our phalanx of women contrasted with Nana's isolation, which I felt as though I shared on the afternoons I went to her house.

We'd eat a tiny dinner together, and I was to save any leftovers. Sometimes I argued that she'd never eat that crust of tarragon chicken salad sandwich or the bottom tablespoon of yogurt she'd push to the back of the fridge and forget. Sometimes I pulled out as evidence two other crusts, or a bit of fuzzed-over cream cheese, and she'd shake her head and say: "I just don't like to waste."

"But these are wasted. See, I'm throwing them away." It felt like bullying. But to keep putting in and throwing away felt like letting myself be manipulated.

"Don't let me see you do it," she said.

Then I attended to the day's tasks. *She* wanted a bulb replaced in the entryway and the hot-water level checked in the ancient boiler in the basement. *I* wanted to put in Wi-Fi so that I could access the Internet. By converting her bills to electronic, I hoped to slow the paper avalanche that had taken over the dining room. Alone during the day, she'd begin to tackle old notices and reorganize them into the many supermarket produce and shopping bags that rolled off the table and onto the floor like tumbleweed. By the time I arrived, she fairly shook with anxiety and confusion. *I* wanted to consult a lawyer about a slip-and-fall lawsuit working its way, *Bleak House*-like, through Philadelphia's courts; *she* wanted to forget about it.

"Now *that* you can throw away!"

She wanted me to take out the envelopes she'd hidden in Pop-Pop's old sock drawer. (Now I understood the cliché—socked away!) Those on the left side were labeled for "Business"; those on the right were hers, labeled, in her handwriting, in caps: THE PROPERTY OF LORENE H. JACKSON. She wanted me to bring the money to the kitchen table where she could count it, and I could check her. She could barely see, and her movements were slow. She wanted all the money laid out—tens of thousands of dollars—to count and arrange in piles and replace into the envelopes. Like a wheelchair gangster, with me cast as the underling.

"Now, here: you check me. How many is that? Am I right?"

"Am I right?"

"No."

"Let's do it again."

Funky, dirty-bill smell diffused through the kitchen. That's how she wanted it. She claimed that having the money on hand made her feel safe. Except that she lived in fear of theft, so that the list of who were allowed into the house got very short. I felt my choke chain tightening.

"What if something happens and I need cash?" She elongated the final digraph—*shhhhh*.

"Cashmoney, cashmoney," I'd answer her, trying to make light. "Sure, Nana." Inevitably, she'd reference the Great Depression and divorce. I heard it, but without compassion. "But how much do you need, Nana? Could you do with me putting, let's say, just this thousand into the bank this week?"

"How much will that leave me?"

"Twenty-five. Nana, surely you don't need more than twenty-five thousand dollars' cash in the house with you in Pop-Pop's underwear drawer."

"Oh, stop it! When you put it like that, go ahead."

We did this ritual over nearly a year until she was down to two thousand ca*shhhh*, in case of a zombie apocalypse, when, I know, I know, money means nothing anyway . . .

The year after Nana Jackson died, I heard social psychologists claiming on the radio that seeing and handling paper money can release endorphins that ease pain and anxiety, and I remembered how she'd sit back, relaxed, after these counting sessions, and sigh, and begin to clean up for dessert.

But the certain way to ease anxiety was love. When my sister and daughter and I came into her bedroom that summer night from the family reunion, not sure whether she'd be alive or dead, Nana managed to find some secret cache of life force under her bed, pop it into her mouth, and swallow it down with a sip of the water that was still where I'd left it from the night before. Then she pulled a century-old Brownie smile out from her pocket and spread it across her face.

"Carole here and Laura, too?" Well, of course she could sit up, yes!

Then, with the lights on and the TV off, she claimed to feel a little better. And, yes, now that we were here, she'd drink some more water. All we lacked was our eighth-grade daughter Zoë, and why hadn't I brought her?

Because I didn't want her to see you dead, was the real answer, but I said: "You didn't answer the phone, Nana, so we were worried."

We found the landline, off the hook where she'd knocked it, and when we got a dial tone, called the ambulance. We told her it was coming.

But she wasn't going to the hospital. Oh, no. There was gravel and grit in the refusal.

To offset the anger, Nana managed an ancient coquetry, nearly giggling about how she'd been very bad about drinking more water, but now that we were here, she could, and she was feeling just the tiniest bit better.

And besides she wasn't going.

"Now, you haven't said anything about the reunion and how it all went. And how did Zoë like meeting her relatives?"

When the EMTs came up the groaning stairs, they filled the bedroom with loud young, white, male bodies and voices. Brusque, competent, cheery. Their practice was simply to pick her up, put her on the gurney, strap her down, and carry her out. Since we wanted agreement and not just compliance, however, we asked them to slow down a bit. My sister suggested they use a chair rather than a stretcher so Nana could sit erect and feel less vulnerable. And, we said, since she was seventy years their senior, they were not to call her by her first name. When she was strapped and ready to go, I told Nana that one of us would ride in the ambulance with her.

This would *kill her*, she rasped at me, and it would be on my head!

"Okay, Nana," I said, repeating her Renaissance language, "on my head be it."

But it would also be on my head—and in my head, and in my family's—I thought, if we left her to die alone lying in a tablespoon of her own urine.

Two days later the antibiotic boosted Nana's 100-year-old immune system to fight off the infection. Intravenous hydration was restoring her energy and mental sharpness. I went back and forth between home and the hospital with Zoë, who stayed for hours next to Nana's bed zipping through her new Harry Potter. At night I took Zoë home and returned to sleep in Nana's room to reassure her when she awoke confused and to help her onto the bedpan. By the third day she was able to shuffle to the bathroom herself, and at bedtime, insisted I go home to my family. I tied the nurse's call button to the side of her bed and we practiced to make sure she could remember and reach it. She'd be fine, she said.

"You just go home and get a good night's sleep."

It was the same tone of voice she'd used for years as she engineered one after another work-around since the dose of arthritis medicine that gave her one miraculous pain-free day—followed by weakness that put her into a wheelchair. Ten years before, I had picked one up at a yard sale for a trip we took to DC. She tried to forbid my taking it, as if having it near would bring on debility. I insisted that it was my car and technically my wheelchair, and I could throw into the back hatch whatever I liked. Then, when she saw the quarter-mile-long line into the White House—and the special rear wheelchair entrance with no line—she agreed. With toddler Zoë in a backpack carrier and Nana in the wheelchair, I approached a tall, uniformed young black military man who asked respectfully whether Nana could stand while he inspected the chair.

"Oh, yes, I can stand. I'm only in this old thing because of the line . . ."

"Yes, ma'am," he said, extending his arm to help her sit again, and to readjust the foot pedals.

"Well," Nana said as we passed the next few good-looking young men in uniforms, "if I had known it would be like that, I would have given in to the chair ten years ago!"

Eventually, we procured an upstairs chair for her house— a thin, lightweight new one and left the old one downstairs. When I'd leave after a visit, she accompanied me to the door in her wheelchair so that I would not see her go upstairs backwards on her bottom, dragging herself up, step-by-step, with her arms. Later, I waited until she was upstairs, having ascended by way of our rigged three-level pillow routine, off the floor onto the bed, and then into the upstairs wheelchair. I'd leave, putting the downstairs chair in exactly the right position at the bottom of the stairs, brakes on, knowing that in case of emergency, she would never get down quickly. In case of fire, she'd burn. In case of forced entry, she'd be completely, utterly vulnerable.

"Good night, dear."

I'd lock the door, and remind myself that I had influence, but no control. Then, on the drive home, across the Delaware, I'd say the Serenity Prayer or play *Aïda* or reggae and sing very loudly until I'd dragged myself back up to where she lived, as old people say in recovery groups, on the banks of the river called De Nile.

But after this last body blow and hospitalization, it seemed unlikely that any miracle would ever get her back into her house.

∼

It smelled grassy-green on the early summer evening I drove away from Our Lady of Lourdes hospital, nearly flying with freedom, even though I knew that I'd be talking to my husband about Nana's moving in with us later this week. After that there would be no more free nights like this one. I treasured that night, thinking happily what to cook for dinner.

It was taken down for months for renovations after an earthquake, but that night the Blessed Virgin Mary statue pulled herself up to her full thirty-foot height and turned on her three-foot-tall halo in the twilight just for me. We'd made fun of her ridiculous neon corona for years. But this night, I lay down the burden of worrying. Worrying that the old boiler would malfunction and Nana would burn up or freeze, that she'd slip, or that she would knock the landline downstairs off the hook again and be unable to call from the one upstairs, that the regular on-off of the lights would give burglars perfect intelligence for forced entry, and that she'd have no defense.

This night, the static of worry quieted. I let the glory roll down on me. Next to the road, in the Catholic graveyard, fireflies floated silently, happy and golden in the twilight, trying to get laid.

⌒

Early on in our relationship, before we were married, I told Bob that although he wanted to marry me, he might not have considered the down-the-road vista. I was a black woman to whom being black had mattered urgently ever since I could remember. Marrying me would mean he'd be all bunched up into one flesh with black America. I could not be with someone who wouldn't take on faith that white supremacy had seeped into the drinking water. That he hadn't noticed and often still didn't see meant I'd ask him to step over to my side of street and not dismiss my whacky, nappy perceptions in favor of some "larger" truth. He said he was open to learn.

Speaking of black, I told him, there was also my small, but often demanding, family, including alcoholics—mostly functional, but still. And we had lots of shades and varieties of black experience to live with. There were the Caribbean descendants, insistent on protocol, though not quite as courteous as Barbados still is, with its roadside signs urging pleases and thank-yous. There were the descended-from-free-people-of-color North Carolina side, Nana's people. Both sides had their divorces and anger, like sunken ships; we have our egos and outsized ambitions, secrets and lies, and running throughout all of it, on both sides like marbled meat, impossible boundaries, trespassed, ignored, beaten down, and in their place, walls erected instead.

On my mother's side were cousins whom he would meet

soonest, because they were my favorites, including the couple who'd shown me when I was a teenager that inter-racial marriage was possible and often funny. ("So I go to the hotel," my cousin Stephanie would say in her New York accent, "and I say 'I'm Mrs. Eamon Tuscano,' and you should see their faces . . .")

At one of the first gatherings Bob attended with my mother's family, my aunt decided, after a Scotch or two, that she would be the one to crack his white, Midwestern, introvert reserve, to make him open up, spill his guts, tell all. Having failed, she stood in the middle of the living room and asked in her I'm-calling-you-out voice: "Bob, how long will it take for me to get to know you?"

His answer, which my maternal grandmother loved to quote for a private chuckle: "Decades . . . But I'll be around."

When my mother, with her premium on expressivity, instructed him on how to hug her properly, that he shouldn't stand there all stiff, but should put his arms around her like this—flopping them up onto her waist—he replied that where he came from, if you hug folks too close, it could mean you wanted to go to bed with them. My mother shouted what became her Bob tagline: "He will say things that catch you right off guard!"

Besides tribe and kin, there was also me, myself, I warned him, descendant of divorces for two generations before me on both sides. I tended to drop into shame at the least prov-ocation. I smoked and hated myself for it, but couldn't quit. Despite wanting commitment, I was prone to withdrawing from it. I'd already married once, and never became a real partner. I liked being in a pretend world with characters I

made up more than the real world with real people, real conflict, real demands. I suspected, as I told him, that all told,
if he really knew me, he wouldn't love me. It was my deepest
and most honest suspicion, the puddle in the basement that
I kept locked, as if no harm would come from the seeping
dampness.

Bob's answer cracked a door that took years to open: "Let
me try."

As for race and family, he said that he welcomed "the full
catastrophe," a quote he'd loved from *Zorba the Greek*, and
had long wanted to live into, he said.

Still I left for a year to teach at my old boarding school,
St. Paul's, in New Hampshire. When crazy people are about
to do a whack marriage, somebody should send one of 'em
away to boarding school, I told him. Maybe some give-back
to young people would clear my head. Or maybe I'd learn
what had happened in my adolescence to set me up for personal and professional lives that baffled me. I'd married
wrong, written for *Time*, edited for *TV Guide*, and couldn't
tell myself why. Bob had married and divorced twice. He'd
marry anybody, and had done, and was about to do so again!
As he says now: "If Dr. Phil had met us, he would have loudly
advised against it."

At the end of the summer I returned from St. Paul's we
were married at a small house museum outside the city. It
was a quiet ceremony with family and a few friends. My sister, as my maid of honor, walked the few grassy steps from
the house to the big tree where the minister waited with

Bob and his son Geoffrey. Reverend Joan Charles had not done many weddings yet. Recently ordained, she'd been at my African Methodist Episcopal church for years and had convinced the adult members of the gospel choir to let me sing with them when I was twelve. We knelt before her under a tree, an unlikely pair on a Civil War-era blanket we weren't sure we were allowed to use. Not one person attending suspected that Bob would follow Reverend Charles into second-career ministry from his work as a magazine editor.

Here we were, more than twenty years later, in the rectory, where Bob had already told me we could accommodate Nana if necessary. Although we would often think of this as the next phase of Nana's life, it was for us another step into "full catastrophe," after children, and writing, my founding Art Sanctuary and his attending seminary. It was another commitment to more-than-you-know, that constant state of being for which Saint Paul, likely imprisoned in Rome, wrote his dedication to the church at Ephesus: "Now to him whose power working within us is able to do infinitely more than we can ask or imagine . . ." We would need that power, all of us, including two daughters who had no say, but like children always and everywhere, must walk the road their parents and grandparents and great-grandparents choose. Nana's coming would be another try at saying yes to life, as someone in Bob's California Bay-area past had liked to declare, or in this case, as if anyone had a choice, saying yes to death.

Chapter 2

The next morning when I went to the hospital, Nana's sheets were soaked with urine. I tried to make light of it, but gently, because both of us knew how humiliated she felt, and how cold and dirty. "Aw, Nana, we finally got you able to pee . . ."

I checked the call button, wondering whether she hadn't been able to grab it fast enough. Had she forgotten?

"That thing doesn't work," she said in disgust.

I pressed. Sure enough, the panel behind the bed failed to light. I ran my hand along the cord to feel for cracks. The cord was fine—but it had come out of the wall. It lolled stupidly on the bed rail, tied, as I'd left it. Someone other than Nana had yanked it out of its socket. Maybe after she'd pushed it I don't know how many times and said God knows what to them when they finally arrived. Or when someone left her on the bedpan to care for someone else. Or called her by her first name. I stood stunned for a minute, smelling the urine, holding the call-button plug in my hand, trying not to hear the voice of my maternal aunt Laura, a nurse, speaking dismissively in her New York accent about some nurses who choose the night shift "and then get mad when the people wake up!" If Nana went into a nursing home, I thought, this is how it would be.

"I'm wet." Shame tinged the rage a shade darker.

Once she'd begun to have problems getting up, making one and then another left turn around the beds in her house, and across the hall to the bathroom, Nana used a bucket at night, a regular mop bucket, next to her night table. She removed and then replaced a piece of cardboard over the top. It wasn't great, but she resisted any other solution. A potty chair would have required moving her bed to be closer to the door, so that was a definite no.

For months after the worn plastic interior of her bucket could no longer be bleached or baking soda'd back to odorlessness, Nana refused to okay the purchase of a new bucket. One day, tired of the smell, I bought a brand-new bucket and took the old one out for trash pickup. For weeks, she couldn't decide what outraged her more: that I'd overreached, or wasted the cost of a new bucket.

Standing next to her bed in the hospital, I wanted to go find the nurse-supervisor and show her that the call-button cord had been yanked out. But I couldn't leave Nana to marinate in a wet bed wishing she were home with her bucket, covered by an old legal pad.

"Here, help me to the bathroom."

On the door was a sign in thick black letters: FALL RISK.

Nana squinted at it. "What does that say about me?"

"Just their warnings against falling."

They'd put the same designation on a bracelet around her wrist. When I rolled the IV stand to one side and lent her my arm, she stood, flat-footed, mouth set, as if to give the lie to their signs.

Well, of course she was a fall risk! Nana had been a fall risk for years. Could have been one of her many names: Rosalie Lorene Hagans "Fall Risk" Cary Jackson. And only God knew how many times she'd done fall-down-go-boom and never told. After self-rehabbing from the not-a-stroke, Nana began to refer to the residual weakness in her arm as "tennis elbow." If you pointed out that she'd never played tennis, she'd just let out a big old laugh. Nana had worked so hard to hold on to the ways we know ourselves as adults: we breathe on our own, toilet ourselves, move about of our own volition, communicate with others, fix and eat food, handle money, live where we choose. She'd been struggling each day to succeed.

In one night she'd lost it all.

The social worker would not let her move back to her home alone, of course, and wondered whether we had a Plan B.

⁓

A day or two later, the medical bureaucracy launched from watch-and-wait to warp drive, and Nana was coming into our household fast enough to blow our eyebrows off. On the morning Nana was dismissed, the social worker ordered her put on home hospice care with an attentive and holistic

Catholic service provider near us. We'd need a hospital bed. It arrived at the house before I did. The social worker gave me information on two companies that installed chair rails. Both sent salespeople pronto to explain to me how to buy a new chair rail or rent a used one. We set her up in the long parlor on the second floor. Nana's hospital bed was on the east wall, and next to it her night table that we brought from her house in New Jersey. I slipped her wallet into the top drawer, the glasses from the low-vision clinic, and other things, as she thought of them, that she wanted close at hand. The drawer pull sounded its familiar metal-hinge creak before hitting the wood as she reached, over and over, to open the drawer, feel around to do an inventory, and then closed it.

I worked with Nana to find the best position for the new potty chair. Perpendicular to the night table worked best; she could stand and turn and sit. Hand wipes perched on top of the night table with a tiny trash receptacle underneath. When I'd leave the room, I'd hear her practicing—standing, turning, and sitting. Or she'd be memorizing the contents of the drawer, laying things in a pattern and feeling them before putting them back. It was like a slo-mo present-moment yoga/haiku exercise:

> *From bed to chair and*
> *Back again. Not where they were.*
> *But where they are now.*

> *I liked how things were:*
> *Habit kept Death at bay. Change*
> *Has kicked in the door.*

On the other side of the long room was a parlor setting: a couch, a bureau for her clothing, a folding table and chairs for when we brought a meal up to her room, and a television.

Barbara, the hospice nurse, visited within a day. At first Nana wanted nothing to do with her. Zero. Medical people asked her the same questions, over and over. Hadn't anyone written down the answers? Didn't they have carbon paper anymore? Didn't they have computers for Barbara to see? Same damn questions. Nurse Barbara spoke to her with deference, and Nana answered in swallowed monosyllables. She told Nurse Barbara that she couldn't see the use of it.

Barbara was not deterred, thank the Lord. Well, then, she asked, what would Nana like to talk about? Nana told her about her father, who had raised five children after his wife's death after childbirth. She told Barbara that her father had died in his sleep. She said it, as usual, in a defiant, perfect-death haiku:

> *He ate his supper,*
> *Went to bed, and then, next day,*
> *He didn't get up.*

"And that's how you'd like it, too," Nurse Barbara said. She voiced simple compassion, clear-eyed, practiced, never complicated by pity.

Nana grunted an acknowledgment.

"Well, I can't promise you that, but I can work with you and your family to try to see how peaceful we can make it."

Finally, Nana let Barbara examine her, and as she ran her hand over Nana's back, Barbara marveled at the smoothness and suppleness of her skin. Nana said that they all just liked to flatter her.

When Barbara left, Nana implied that she must have been impressed by the rectory.

"In the rectory" was how we referred to Nana's stay, not to aggrandize the stone neocolonial, but to recognize that it had been donated to the church in 1924 by a local bishop; in other words, it wasn't ours. We were installed there to serve the Memorial Church of the Good Shepherd. Our own house, our "real house," was a sixteen-foot-wide row house in South Philadelphia which we were renting to young friends of the family.

"In the rectory" signaled the boundaries I tried to draw on the arrangement we were entering into. My cousin Dana had lived "in the rectory" with us for a while when her mid-career switch led her to nursing school in her forties. So the phrase had a history; it acknowledged the independence of a grown woman choosing for a time to live in a space large enough to accommodate the priest, his wife and daughter and dog, with stop-ins by a recent college grad daughter and occasional summer visits from Bob's son and family, our grandchildren, Sam and Zach, from Texas.

Dana had stopped over with us on her way to somewhere else: graduation, work, a relationship with a hardworking and loquacious building contractor, in a tiny, Martha Stewart house on a narrow Philadelphia street that bore her mother's first name. For Nana, though, this was the terminus, her last stopover. Before what?

My husband, usually called Father Bob in the parishes he's served, says that many worship communities agree not to specify exactly what happens after death. People sit next to one another in the pews thinking, feeling, intuiting, or assuming, widely, even wildly, different deaths and after-deaths: from wings and a crown, to rest, to oblivion, to straight-up dust.

What did Nana believe? Don't get me to lying. For all the time we spent together, intimately, and despite my farcical attempts to create for Nana as much in-house independence as possible, I cannot say what she hoped for or feared. But she did fear. In fact, Nana was terrified.

Living in the rectory, with vestry and prayer meetings, a weekly in-house mass service and children's gatherings, gave her gladness, just as the fireplace dispelled the gloom of winter. But none of it brought ultimate comfort, or what the funeral mass terms "sure and certain hope." Nana liked knowing that she had "a priest in the family," which she said as if he were a possession. My sister Carole joked that Nana was, as Madonna sang, "a material girl." So how was she to imagine the extinguishing of the body?

"What does Bob say?" she asked me after Barbara told us that hospice was for people expected to live no longer than six months. Nana asked me, almost in the same breath, to take particular care after she died of the Chinese jardinières on the fireplace mantel, because these were probably worth the most of all her best things.

"Bob says that God is love," I said, ignoring the jardinière directive.

Nana sighed.

Chapter 3

Wide windows to the east and west brought in light from dawn through twilight, and two sets of double French doors on either side of the fireplace on the south wall opened onto the roof over the porch downstairs. It wasn't a deck per se, but on that first early evening we used it as one. Nana and I rolled out onto the roof and sat as if in the trees, "halfway to heaven." She laughed lightly at her own lyricism before she withdrew into silence.

The young boys next door delighted in the spectacle. They shouted touching, well-mannered questions: "How did you get up there?" "How are you feeling today?" "Is it fun to sit up high?" I relayed what they said and what they were doing; then I called down to them Nana's answers. At dinner she repeated the conversation as if she'd seen and heard them herself.

Nana began a running conversation about these new neighbors: Darryl Ford and his wife Gail, and their two boys. He was the first black headmaster of Penn Charter, the school begun by William Penn. Gail was an obstetrician. We watched and commented on the trucks bringing tents and caterers to the head-of-school's house on days before donor parties and alumni and trustee gatherings.

To the Fords, Nana's next-door rooftop presence was a reminder of family members in pleasantly named Buena Vista, Virginia. Cousin Irma, whom they called Mama Irma, was just a few years younger than Nana. Nana brought her to mind because Darryl's family passed on "a story about Irma standing on the roof of her house and doing a dance and shouting how much she loved Johnny, the man who would become her husband." He also recalled how the town had a "two-room schoolhouse for African Americans" that many of his family went to. Like Nana's sister Flora, Mama Irma taught school: black children, of course. Now Darryl says: "The school is designated a historic site; however, it has been hard to raise the small amount of money to finish the restoration. While many African Americans value the education and love they received at the 'colored school,' they see it as a symbol of all that was unjust about education in the South."

Darryl's older family members would have recognized Nana's family: her father, William Scarlett Hagans, and his brother Henry Edward, whom I almost never heard about. Professor Henry Hagans presided over the Goldsboro, North Carolina, State Colored Normal School and would have recognized the Reconstruction-era mission to educate black youth properly and well in segregated schools with little money. The Hagans brothers were race men, enthusiastic Republican warriors for the gains to be made from sharing control of local and federal offices. But from the time his parents nicknamed him "Snow Bee," my great-grandfather added looking white as the subtext to his stories of life as a turn-of-the-twentieth-century Race Man.

Nana was also able to pass for white. When she took me to Philadelphia's Academy of Music with her, back before white folks showed off their Obama-like grands, I was Nana's racial marker. She sewed me red-and-blue tartan outfits from fabric she bought on motor trips, as she called them, to Nova Scotia. The plaids matched perfectly, and she steamed in sharp creases and clasped the edge with a bronze kilt safety pin. Like ladies we glided into the red-velvet and gold-leaf hush of the Academy of Music to Nana and Pop's subscription seats. On these nights Pop stayed home, where Nana said he could doze for free in front of the TV.

In the academy, people looked back and forth between Nana and me to assess us for race, class, and relationship. I took from this color means nothing, except for what people think it means. Not just at the academy, but everywhere. Throughout my childhood, when I was with Nana, people studied the outward signs of our breeding as if they were judges from the Westminster Kennel Club, and we were, you know: there was my short, fuzzy hair, pulled back as tight and straight as Mommy's formidable skills could get it, and Nana's doll-baby-straight auburn bun; our different noses and the matching freckles splattered over them; and her complete lack of discomfort under their gaze. So many of Nana and Pop-Pop's family and friends looked white that

I assumed the world of white-looking people I saw on the streets and in the media included even more than the 25 percent some biologists claim must have recent African ancestry (as opposed to the African Eve, mother of us all).

The main difference between black and white, it seemed to me, must have to do with qualities that I could not articulate but maybe could sense. Google images of actress Fredi Washington in the 1934 tearjerker film *Imitation of Life*. Or new British duchess Meghan, wife of Harry. If you grew up with these people, how would race read? Because I responded emotionally to the piano playing of Van Cliburn, for instance, and because Nana's record album showed him to have wavy hair like Daddy's, to me, Cliburn was black. And Rosalind Russell, of course; Bette Davis (those eyes, that attitude); and Ava Gardner playing *Show Boat* in Lena Horne's role, natch. Clergymen I saw on television marching for civil rights; they cared when others didn't, so I just figured them to be black, like the Episcopal priest who baptized me.

At the Academy of Music, when people checked us out, Nana withdrew into inaccessible reaches of herself, and every now and then returned to pat my hand. I never asked how she felt when they stared. We sat in our regular seats, and the music began. Conductor Eugene Ormandy, a small gray man in tails, would climb up onto his stand and conduct, so far as I can remember, without a score. I'd close my eyes and wonder how it might feel to keep the music of every single instrument in mind at once. Sometimes, despite the music, my mind daydreamed and I heard other sounds: church songs, the bumpity hum of my bicycle tires on cement, or my maternal great-grandfather's musical, Caribbean voice.

Or I imagined the lives of Nana's family when they got to Philadelphia just before World War I, in the black-and-white photos she let me see. Four sisters and one brother sit in two rows under a tree. In one, Nana smiles from the lower left with long, wavy hair pulled back in a half ponytail, looking very young in contrast to her sisters. In another, I see her soon after she and her brother were let out of quarantine for scarlet fever. Then, she said, back before antibiotics, wasn't like it is now. Scarlet fever wiped out whole families, so she knew that the quarantine was necessary. Her full head of brown hair is shaved close. Why would they shave off her hair? I asked repeatedly. Nana shook her head and smiled at my consternation. "You know, honey, I don't really know. That's just what they did. I guess they thought they had to."

This was a few years before the famous photos of the Russian czarinas Romanov, heads shaved after they contracted measles during the epidemic in 1917, a year and a half before their assassinations. Throughout my childhood, when I studied the photos, I yearned for Nana's glorious mane of wavy hair, wondering, like other black girls who drank America's good-hair Kool-Aid, how I would feel with that growing from my scalp instead of my never-long-enough brown naps.

That's all she said about getting scarlet fever. Except for one part, her favorite. Nana remembered that once she and her brother began to recover, someone sent Temple oranges that she was to share with him. I'm never sure how far from her was the separate boys' ward, but this much is clear: the bag of oranges came to her, and it was her responsibility, because she was older, to divvy them up. But she ate one first, and it tasted so juicy and sweet, she said, that she hid the bag under the covers—and ate them all herself. Each time she repeated the story, I was scandalized. The older sister was duty-bound to look out for the younger kids. But she wasn't the oldest, she reminded me. Of the girls she was the baby, the one who lost her mother as a child.

On our leisurely weekends, I asked Nana questions to try to elicit her stories in long form. What she gave, what my father gave later, were nubs, thumbnails, beats. Example: "My one memory of my mother was her sending me into the field to pick cotton to stuff a doll she was making for me."

The family came north the year Nana turned six. Soft cotton bursts the boll in the fall, but sharp spurs on the tips stick the fingers even of experienced pickers. Other hazards: cockle burrs in the rows stick to clothing; saw briars cut the legs and feet; and various insects, including the notorious pack saddle, bite and sting. Would Nana's mother, Lizzie E. Burnett, wife of a landowner, even if she were busy with other children, have sent six- or five- or four-year-old Nana into a cotton field to harvest even a few tiny handfuls of cotton alone? Did Lizzie grow ornamental cotton near the house just for this purpose, as our own neighbors did in Pennsylvania. ("Every child oughta know *cotton!*" said Aunt Bea from Georgia, wife of Uncle Fletcher, who believed that pure tobacco never hurt anybody, but that "devilish filters" were causing lung cancer.)

But, back to Lizzie: suppose she grew just enough cotton to make dolls, like we grow herbs in pots by our back doors in the city. Would she have sent a young child out to get her finger pricked and, as one of my granddaughters says, "cry-cry-cry"?

Once I had my own daughters, and once I had studied cotton to write books about the South, these were my new questions. But throughout my childhood, Nana repeated the same story, almost word for word. When we sewed dolls together, when we admired dolls in stores or catalogues; or when she said, as she often did, that she should have started a doll collection like her friend whose husband owned a gas station; and when I answered, as I no longer wanted dolls myself, that she still could.

Another example: Nana said that her father enrolled the oldest daughter, Susan, whom they called Babe, in a black boarding school, and because she later found somebody to elope with, he never allowed any of the younger children to go away to school. When they came to Philadelphia, richer with black society by far than Wayne County, North Carolina, William Hagans would only allow them to join one club, because he considered these girl clubs frivolous, unlike his political or self-help societies. Nana said, as if I knew anything about World War I-era black society: "Papa always said that one club was enough for anyone." She never remembered their names.

My dad inherited Will Hagan's hunting guns. Dad made a case for them to hang on the wall in our three-room apartment: carved wood lined with green felt. It looked to me as if he'd fashioned an altar from a pool table. Despite allergies and a love of animals, Dad loaded these ancestral hunting guns into the car for the adventure of occasional solo hunting days in the Pennsylvania woods. Also, I supposed, as an act

LORENE CARY

of reverence, as if he were creating for himself an ancestry narrative to carry him back beyond the father who disappointed him. He would refer throughout my childhood to the father who failed him. This stern grandfather hadn't.

Dad brought home more live animals than dead ones— our favorite dog Duchess, the Irish setter who ran after the car until he stopped and brought her home; the pheasant with the broken leg he splinted and kept in the basement until it healed. Soon, Dad began practicing judo, the sport he made his own from beginning grade through black belt over nearly fifty years. Wrestling and ritual suited him better than killing animals.

While the rest of African Americans struggled through the self-naming exercises of the sixties, Nana characterized her racial heritage as a "League of Nations." She pronounced it with a little leftover North Carolina gargle in her throat: "Ligga Nations," which I couldn't understand, like opera lyrics, but felt. Ligga Nations was clearly a way to sidestep the given categories, but my mind could not stop playing with language. Ligga Nations rhymed, couldn't help it, with Nigga Nations. It was also a phrase that pissed my mother off, I could tell, as did the Southern-accented moments at Easter when one of the Hagans siblings in their sixties would start polishing the Golden Age of Hagans, with land references and the inevitable phrase: "Well, it was a plantation, really. I mean that's what it was . . ."

There'd be a moment of family trance, when they'd all smile at each other—Aunt Susie, Aunt Flora, and Nana—

44

like the three pastel fairies in Disney's animated *Sleeping Beauty*. They shared secrets we could not know: the life from South to North; slipping into and out of census categories of colored, mulatto, and white every ten years; losing touch mostly with a sister who'd gone north, they said, to pass. It's an experience I've not known, this walking abroad in America wearing faux white skin like a cloak of visibility. And their experiences of the stern Will S. Hagans differed with birth order. Nana, the youngest girl, held the rosiest, while the oldest, Susan, remembered being thrust into housekeeping at thirteen after her mother's death. It was as if they were from different families.

Not everyone descended from William Scarlett Hagans felt the existential estrangement of our branch. Other cousins have happily shared info gathered by Lisa Y. Henderson, a distant relative who is a regional attorney for the National Labor Relations Board's Atlanta office by day—and black genealogical superhero by night. Her websites include Fourth Generation Inclusive (ncfpc.net) and Scuffalong.com. The material there has introduced me to William Scarlett Hagans on his own terms.

Born in 1869, Nana's father learned to walk and talk as the federal government forced North Carolina and other rebel states to remove legal slavery from their Constitutions. At the same time, the Fifteenth Amendment to the US Constitution banned any infringement on a male citizen's right to vote "on account of race, color, or previous condition of servitude." Hagans grew up prosperous and free, the son of a free, but illiterate father, Napoleon, who eventually owned nearly five hundred acres of land near Aycock Swamp in Wayne County.

In 1880, Napoleon testified before the US Senate—Will would have been twelve and his brother Henry thirteen. This from Senate Report 693, 2nd session, 46th Congress: [The Senate wanted to investigate] ". . . *the Causes of the Removal of the Negroes from the Southern States to the Northern States.*"

Because whyever would black people want to leave Dixie?

NAPOLEON HIGGINS [*sic*], colored, sworn and examined. By North Carolina Senator [Zebulon Baird] Vance [whose bio reflected the century from the white side: former slave owner, Confederate officer, governor of North Carolina, prisoner, governor again, then senator]:

Question: Where do you reside? —Answer: Near Goldsborough. I don't stay in Goldsborough, but it is my county seat. I live fifteen miles from town.

Q: What is your occupation? —A: I am farming.

Q: Do you farm your own land? —A: Yes, sir.

Q: How much do you own? —A: Four hundred and eighty-five acres.

Q: How did you get it? —A: I worked for it.

Q: Were you formerly a slave? —A: No, sir; I was a free man before the war.

. . .

Q: What did you pay for it? —A: I believe I paid $5,500;

46

LADYSITTING

and then I have got a little town lot there that I don't
count; but I think it is worth about $500.

. . .

Q: How much cotton do you raise? —A: I don't raise as
much as I ought to. I only raised fifty-eight bales last
year.

Q: What is that worth? —A: I think I got $55 a bale.

Q: How many hands do you work yourself? —A: I generally rent my land. I only worked four last year, and
paid the best hand, who fed the mules and tended
around the house, ten dollars; and the others I paid
ten, and eight, and seven . . . I gave them rations; and
to a man with a family I gave a garden patch and a
house, and a place to raise potatoes.

You can almost hear the attitude. He had everything the
white men had: except education and power. If he gave his
sons the former, they could go after the latter themselves.
Both Will and Henry went to Howard University, with Will
staying on for the college and law departments while Henry
returned to Shaw University in Raleigh. Napoleon also had
a child out-of-wedlock with his wife's twin sister. Will and
Henry's half brother, Joseph, whom I heard mentioned a few
times throughout my childhood, went to medical school and
moved west.

Eight years before Nana was born, her father William Hagans
inherited his half of Napoleon's more than 485 acres of land,
and as secretary to North Carolina's African American con-

gressman George Henry White, attended a reception at the Taft White House. Nana said that her father wrote White's speeches. Maybe he also helped draft that first bill ever proposed to stop lynching in January 1900.

But in a sustained campaign that historian Jan Carew calls "total war," the Jim Crow Democrats and their supporters clawed back control, using laws, voter suppression, books and songs depicting black inferiority, and a campaign of terror. In 1898, just a hundred miles south of the Haganses, in Wilmington, North Carolina, two thousand armed white men carried out the only successful coup d'état in American history. They killed between fifteen and sixty citizens, burned homes, businesses, and the city's black newspaper, and overthrew the legally elected biracial slate of leaders. Did the state or federal authorities return the legally elected representatives? No.

The next year, 1900, poll tax and the grandfather clause kept most blacks from voting. It stayed that way until after I was a girl. With his constituency disenfranchised, Congressman White did not run for reelection. He was the last black member of the House of Representatives until 1929; then, flipping the final two digits, the last from North Carolina until 1992.

A short documentary about the life of Congressman White ends with a clip of President Barack Obama quoting White's last speech in the House in 1901 to the Congressional Black Caucus: "And at the end of an inspiring farewell address, the gentleman from North Carolina said, 'This, Mr. Chairman, is perhaps the Negro's temporary farewell to the

American Congress. But let me say, phoenix-like, he will rise up someday and come again.'"

Nana would have loved to see that.

White was pushed out of government, and the South. He moved his family to Washington, DC, then Philadelphia, where he founded the People's Savings Bank, the first black-owned bank in the city. He also helped found Whitesboro, New Jersey, the town Nana nodded at as we sped by each year going to the Jersey shore.

Perhaps following White's lead, Will Hagans moved his family to Philadelphia in 1913. Their names continued to show up on the Northern versions of their self-help and racial uplift initiatives. During her first year in Philadelphia, Nana's mother Lizzie gave birth to a stillborn boy and died soon after of complications. Mother and child were buried in a family plot in Eden Cemetery, bought in 1902 by a group of black men, including former Congressman White. Throughout that century, as the city rolled over other small black graveyards, Eden reinterred their remains. One of them was Olive Cemetery, which I discovered in *The Underground Railroad*, by conductor William Still, and chose for a scene in my novel *The Price of a Child*. Still is buried in Eden. So is Congressman White, contralto Marian Anderson, Philadelphia Museum of Art architect Julian Abele, "Father of Gospel Music" Charles Tindley, *Philadelphia Tribune* newspaper founder Christopher Perry, Civil War Colored Troops veterans, and Reggie Bryant, founder of the National Black

Journalist Association, one of the few people buried there, other than Nana, whom I've known in the flesh.

It's shushy once you pass the iron gates into Eden. Lawn mowers drone in the spring and the living shuttle at 40 mph from Penn Pines, where my mother and I go for cheap, too-big portions of spaghetti and meatballs, to Collingdale, where we black Yeadon High majorettes knew not to go into the bathrooms at football games unless we wanted a white-girl fight. (And often someone did.)

The souls who have gone, as Nana's generation liked to say, "from labor to refreshment," are not quiet. They and we are still working it. Time circles through Eden in seasons, the liturgical calendar, the births and deaths of family members deposited into their plots one by one. Time is money, and we pay our fees to be cremated or dolled up and buried. But once you step through the gates, time means nothing.

Statement: *God is good.*

Answer: *All the time.*

When I urged Nana to write a will, rather than talk it to me to sort out later, she told me that the way *her* father told it, *his* father, Napoleon "Pole" Hagans, called his sons together, "under the cart shelter." Nana's grandfather told them who would get what land. That conversation had been adequate to hold up in court, a white court, way back then. What he told his sons had been *legally binding*.

From what I can gather, Will Hagans bought out his brother. During the Depression, like so many Americans, Will saw his wealth wiped out. In the last years of his life, he lived with his second wife and her mother in an apartment in West Philadelphia.

My insistence on a will became an insult to Nana's grandfather Napoleon and his land: the effect this illiterate free colored man had on his world, and the caring personal way he distributed it to his sons. Asking her to write a will, she implied, disrespected my ancestors. The old "under the cart shelter" story was my white-looking grandmother's way of playing the dozens; for once, she'd out-blacked me.

The Will Hagans will I came to know governs his trusteeship of a parcel of buildings in South Philadelphia he eventually left for Nana to manage.

Ultimately, Nana did indeed ask her kind lawyer-neighbor-friend Mike to write and execute her will, but for months she remained angry at me for insisting. When I'd ask how she felt, she'd tell me peevishly that "all that harping on death" made her feel ill.

Nana seldom spoke about William Hagans's second wife, Emma L. Titus, but always with respect. Genealogist Henderson summarizes the rest of their lives as follows:

> The Great Depression dealt the couple crippling blows, and William lost his home and other holdings. In the 1940 census of Philadelphia, at 650 57th Street, realtor William Hagans, 65, was renting an apartment for $40/week with wife Emma, 40, a public school teacher, and mother-in-law Ellen Titus, 70.

It may sound like a terrible fall, but he was not destitute, and they lived no worse than many black folks, better than most. William Scarlett Hagans died in 1946 in Philadelphia.

No wonder Nana stuffed her shoe boxes with cash.

And no wonder my mother insisted that we learn, if necessary, to do without.

Chapter 4

The hospice diagnosis was degenerative heart disease. It could be weeks, or as long as six months. My sister and her young family came as often as they could to visit from North Jersey. When they did, Nana sat in her hospital bed in her new nightgown, ordered from L.L.Bean, settling in for imminent death with dignity, encircled by family like a Victorian pen-and-ink illustration.

I told myself that the rectory gave space, and church life, a spiritual container for Nana's end-of-life drama. She reached out into the audience and drew all of us up onstage for crazy improvisation. Like her, I felt out of control, but made certain to try to keep it under wraps. In the evening, I adjusted the sheets and the fan that she wanted to feel on her face, a ritual that took just a few moments, but had to be done exactly the same way each night to help her move from anxiety to restfulness. Often I found myself mumbling Cranmer's Prayer of Thanksgiving:

> And we most humbly beseech thee, O heavenly
> Father, so to assist us with thy grace, that we may . . .

do all such good works as thou hast prepared for us to walk in.

The words had captured my imagination when I was a girl, just learning to lie back and swing in the hammock of worship and poetry, right about when my maternal great-grandmother died, and it felt as if that whole side of the family was tumbling into emotional free fall. After Gramm-mom, what good works were there prepared for us to walk in? We were flailing in mud. My mother still said she didn't need friends because she had sisters, but they argued every single week, it felt like; at the same time my maternal grand-mother's drinking took off. Friday nights at Nana Hamilton's rolled downhill toward shouting and name-calling. Some-times they hit each other.

I spent those nights with my great-grandfather, a thin, lonely, nearly blind old man who had lost the wife who was eleven years his junior. He ceded their first-floor bedroom to my other Nana and withdrew to rooms upstairs. On Friday nights, he taught me poems he remembered from his nine-teenth-century childhood. Longfellow's "Psalm of Life" was one. When I was old enough to look it up, I found it as much ridiculed in the twentieth century as it had been beloved in the nineteenth, when Pap had memorized it in his Barbados school room:

> Tell me not, in mournful numbers,
> Life is but an empty dream!—
> For the soul is dead that slumbers,
> And things are not what they seem.

Life is real! Life is earnest!
And the grave is not its goal;
Dust thou art, to dust returnest,
Was not spoken of the soul.

I remembered, out of context, the last lines of some of the stanzas: "Funeral marches to the grave," and "Learn to labor and to wait."

Cranmer's prayer after communion I'd heard more often, and in so many different voices that it felt tattooed inside me: "All such good works" made sense. That God had prepared them for us made sense, just as the rising of the sun at a certain time on the equinox a hundred years from now was already "prepared," although we hadn't yet seen it happen, and would die before it came. But that God had prepared for us to "walk in" good works?

Now, with Nana's diagnosis, hospice time felt like something that had been prepared for us to walk in together. Not necessarily a good work. We might end up with a sloppy improv. Sometimes I felt like the dog, stretching my head and neck onto the ground to smear onto my skin the stink of death coming at us slo-mo. "If I should die before I wake" coming atcha right from childhood, on some internal loop tape broadcasting right from Nana's 100-year-old amygdala. Did it make it easier that it was not even our home, but the rectory, with its own sense of gracious tenancy? I think so. Every stone of the rectory, which we loved, told us that nothing belongs to us. Not even our bodies.

At other times the prayers struck me as lovely anachronisms from European superstition, where people without antibiotics or the Internet tried to find some way to think about life that was better than "nasty, brutish, and short."

Mostly, Nana's coming death brought to mind, especially at bedtime, other deaths. As in a wedding ceremony, where the liturgy instructs you to think of other weddings, and to think of your own and recommit to it, tucking Nana in and feeling her hip bone was the bell that tolled for me to reconnect with my own mortality.

I thought of Pap Drayton frequently, because he'd been my closest and dearest elderly person throughout my childhood, and he'd taught me how he and his superannuated siblings oriented themselves toward death.

By the time I met Pap, he had returned to the Anglican faith of his childhood. It gave him comfort and connected him to his own childhood, as did the folktales he taught me: hogs in the Barbados cornfield; the woman who slips out of her skin at night to fly around the island; the father who tells his daughter to jump, and when she does, lets her fall, just to teach her to trust no man. Telling me brought his childhood to mind, the colonial 1880s, speaking to the American century as it heaved through the 1960s. Reading the boy Samuel with Eli was Pap's way of telling me to listen for the call of God, even as he began to aim himself toward death.

After his wife, Grammom, died, he told me that as a young man he thought he could not survive the loss of his mother. "I cried for her like I could never cry for anyone else." He ached for his wife, plump, brown, attuned to his needs, but he accepted her death, and his loneliness, and his increasing blindness and disability. He would soon leave us, but he could wait.

Aunt Dine, who came to see us in Philadelphia from Barbados, said on her last trip that she'd looked out the plane window and seen Jesus in the clouds. Just like that: she'd looked out and there he was, gazing at her with love.

Well, of course, the grown-ups said, as did Aunt Dine herself, that Jesus was calling her to him, and she'd likely go to him soon. I remember lots of discussion when she was out of earshot.

—Maybe her last visit to us.

—Probably her last plane ride.

—But did he say anything to you?

—Was he close or far away?

—Did he beckon her?

I fastened on the word "beckon," which sounded arcane enough to have emerged from the King James Bible that Pap and I read together. But if Jesus wanted Aunt Dine, with her lilting accent and thin little legs, why was she here, sitting in the kitchen, joyously telling the tale, instead of having slipped away on the plane?

I took from the story that Jesus was assuring Aunt Dine that her death, which had to be coming sooner rather than later, was nothing to fear. Clouds, blue sky, Jesus: what wasn't to like? And that he wanted her to testify to it before she went. She'd live long enough to tell the tale.

But Nana Jackson's evenings could not have Dine's blessed assurance, because Nana did not have Aunt Dine's relationship with Jesus. No way he'd pop up outside the window for her. Nana squinted and frowned at the windows to keep whoever she saw there out there.

Uncle Richard, Nana's brother-in-law, had had, if not Aunt Dine's brother-Jesus hookup, at least a lifelong faith and deep love of Episcopal church liturgy. He loved going to church. When he was in the hospital, one of my cousins whom he raised came to visit him. I met her there, only to learn that he was, as they say, actively dying. His feet and legs had gone purple; he could no longer speak, and his eyes were closed. The heart and blood pressure monitors showed a jagged graph depicting what the nurse told us was most likely fear as he realized he was dying.

"Talk to him," she said. "He can probably hear us."

Barbara and I stood on either side of his bed and held his hands, saying things to him until we talked to the ends of what we could think of. Then we said prayers, starting with "Our Father, which art in heaven" and moving through the old Eucharist, the one he most likely favored, beginning with "The Lord be with you. / And with thy spirit." We walked through the mass flat-footed, with one or the other forgetting bits. But we said the words like music whose rhythms he knew better than we. And, sure enough, above his head, the monitors showed the green zigzags slowing, lengthening.

But, despite her praise for the beauty of the old Eucharist, when Bob would ask Nana if she'd like a prayer, she'd pause. Finally, she'd assent to a prayer, "but not a long one."

I even thought of Carl, my taciturn Iowan father-in-law, whose death introduced us to hospice care. A young nurse drove her station wagon through miles of fields of corn and soy, and past thousands of hogs, to visit her dying clients. It was she who first taught us about how the body and mind, which we think of as separate, work together as one organism to grapple with death. Horse and rider exchange places, and the mind must put itself at the service of the body, even as the body expresses its last great process through metaphor.

She gave us brochures that helped us to look out for ways that dying people expressed their orientation toward leaving. They might shed their clothes or ask to be taken out of their rooms, it said, as a way of letting loved ones know that they wanted out of their dying bodies. She meant to prepare us. I was not prepared for the night I went into Carl's bedroom, a week or two before his death, to find this modest man, bedridden, who'd mostly stopped speaking, sitting up on the side of his bed, completely naked. How had he Houdini'd himself out of his pajamas? Pulled himself upright to sit unsupported?

Always a thin man, Carl appeared practically skeletal without pajamas to cover the parchment skin that clung to his bones. His blue eyes looked black in their dark circles, peering back through generations. He asked: "Has Rudy had his supper yet?"

I remembered that Rudy was his oldest brother, who had died years before Bob and I married. Carl was back on the farm where his alcoholic father made life hard, and without an evening meal the night would be long.

"Yes," I assured Carl. "Rudy's had his supper."

Satisfied, he allowed himself to be put back into pajamas and to bed, where he died within a week.

Later, a woman I knew who had gone through Yoruba training was at my house. She told me that she sensed a tall, very thin white man's spirit on the second floor of our home. It concerned her that the vision she received was of a white man who seemed to have attached to the household—and the children. I told her that I was going to figure it was my father-in-law, the quiet, but restless, spirit who loved to hold our daughters on his lap and call them one mid-nineteenth-century nickname after another, like L'il Skeeter and L'il Shaver.

Maybe the death I thought about most often after Nana Jackson's diagnosis was that of my maternal grandmother, Nana Hamilton, who died of heart failure after a late-life drinking career and cigarettes, in addition to caring for her daughter, my aunt, paralyzed by a massive stroke at thirty-two years old. After a few drinks, Nana would claim she intended to reach from her coffin and grab one of her daughters in to keep her company. She did no such thing, but when, in 1986, I made changes to her eulogy on our first computer and added her extravagance and love of her pleasures, the version that appeared on the screen later that night was innocent of all revisions: bland, quiet, good.

My mother tells me that it was I who decided as a child to distinguish them by their last names: Nana Jackson and Nana Hamilton. It feels to me that this let me be my own person, despite bearing each of their names, Lorene and Emily.

I inherited other things, too. Six months after I stopped drinking I distinctly heard Nana Hamilton's voice telling me how glad she was that I'd found a way to do what she couldn't. I'd loved her singing voice, which had a shine on it like tempered chocolate, and retained a naughty shimmer, the potential for fun, just there at the back of her throat. That's the voice I heard distinctly. It was hilarious that I took in the nourishment of this particular paranormal event at a booth in an empty Roy Rogers. The floors were still wet from the morning's first ammonia swab. I was waiting for Reading Terminal Market to open, determined to buy a fresh capon, as Nana Hamilton had favored for Thanksgiving toward the end of her life. I had invited eight or nine newly sober people who'd said at an AA meeting that they'd have nowhere to go for the holiday.

"Just tell me how many," Bob had asked, using his most level, managing editor voice.

I told him eight, but a couple of them brought friends. We served them Nana Hamilton's moist capon and mac-and-cheese, definitely an addict special. ("Lay out three cheeses, and all the butter and milk you think you'll need," she said. "Then double it.") More full-catastrophe.

Each person and each death is unique, said the hospice brochures. Nana and I wrestled each night as she tumbled down the stairs from anxiety to restfulness.

It was during these early days that I began to leave snacks for her to have late at night when she awoke hungry and out-of-kilter in this new house. They became a running joke among the caretakers. The saucer on her night table at bedtime ran the gamut from sweet to very sweet: one tiny fruit, one muffiny-cakey option, and one pie or custard option—three, had to be three, with flavors and textures varied and balanced.

One nurse suggested that there might be too much sugar, and I reminded her that Nana was 100 years old, with no diabetes, and no extra weight. Besides, she was actually getting better.

Chapter 5

We needed help.

Gertrude was a tiny, plump, almost always smiling private-duty nurse who had taken care of my grandfather ten years earlier. Ever since, she'd sent cards for holidays, and brought gifts. Gertrude said that Nana reminded her of her own mother, who had died. I figured Gertrude to be in her late sixties or early seventies, maybe wanting to retire from private-duty nursing, but she'd always told me that if and when Nana needed care, I should ring her first. I did.

Gertrude answered the news of Nana on hospice with a comforting mix of professional calm and personal condolence. A quiet sadness ran counterpoint to her bubbly can-do tone. She wanted to see Nana but said that she had a hard time finding new addresses. I picked her up at her house in New Jersey, just a short distance from Nana's house, and drove her to the rectory, where they had a warm, laughing, tearful reunion.

I listened from downstairs, relieved. The first few days since Nana's move-in had required more than I'd expected: more time, more attention, more talk, more large and small problem-solving, more care. Something always needed adjusting: the television wasn't loud enough; or if it was, she couldn't find the stations she liked.

I'd expected Nana would remain as I thought of her. Ever since Pop's death, she'd been "secret, and self-contained, and solitary as an oyster." It was one of Dickens's phrases for Scrooge, which I remembered not from the volumes in our house that Mom bought, but from the books-by-mail children's abbreviated edition, with colors washed over the old pen-and-ink illustrations. I was sorry that that phrase sprang to mind when I thought of her widowhood, but it did, especially when I shut the front door, locked her in, and walked down the path from the porch between the yew bushes, strong-smelling in the spring, and loaded with poison red berries bright against snow in the winter.

"Oh, they live forever," Nana said of the yews, even before we looked them up, courtesy of the new Wi-Fi, and found that some specimens in Europe had been growing for two thousand years.

I had not noticed the signs of increasing loneliness. How grateful she was for her company: the next-door neighbor Jim, who brought her his homemade meatballs and cut her hair; the back-of-the-house neighbor; Mike, a lawyer, whom she even named as the executor of her will; her niece Jeannie, who wrote and also called her for long, chatty phone visits from Texas. When Nana and I talked about a subject one night and I'd come back a day or two or three later, she'd pick up where we'd left off.

Or, most telling, had I paid closer attention, was the uncharacteristic way she folded after seven years of not speaking to my father. It began after he told her he could not drive her to New Hampshire, where I was receiving an honorary doctorate. He felt ill. That was in the evening before dinner, which he ate most nights with her in New Jersey at six after sitting security with her at her one-woman real estate office in South Philadelphia. Instead of asking what was wrong or how he felt, Nana exploded with her own frustration: he'd been fine that morning! And she wanted to go.

At sixty-two my father had been retired from teaching middle school science for seven years. The next seven he would retire from his mother, who, he shouted, "treated him like a servant."

I wondered whether the split had been supported or even prepared by Dad's then girlfriend. I suspected that she, like my mother, might have felt ambivalence about his fealty to Nana's needs and expectations, her housework, her work to maintain the ramshackle apartments, weekly visiting schedules, holiday rituals. In any event, it happened as his life became more his own with his girlfriend, and Nana's strength declined slowly, but then, she was ninety years old, and how many people at ninety don't lose *un poco* here and there?

Seven years after their fight, when my father had surgery to remove a kidney, Nana asked me how he was doing. She even called for an update. My mother also called. All these people who did not speak to each other. I could not understand them. My mother told me that Nana should call him, my dad, because they needed each other, because no matter the offense, no matter everyone's advanced ages, the mother is always mother. So that afternoon, when Nana asked me to tell Dad how much she was thinking of him, I said no. I'd give her the report, but not do surrogate relationship. She pooh-poohed my scruples. It was just a message. I told her that Dad had used me to carry notes when he and Mom had separated, and I'd never forgiven myself. The note said something about the family car and payments. The next morning he came before school and drove the car away. Mom, my sister, and I had stood at the window and watched.

Nana said I was overdramatic.

I gave her his hospital room and phone number. The next day, when I went to visit, she was there.

Alone no longer worked. She needed company, and she needed it so much that I began to feel swallowed up. If I were to return to work, we had to find help.

Yes, Gertrude said on the ride back from their first visit together, she would love to help. No, she didn't want to talk about money, because she'd already told Nana that she'd give her a reduced rate, since Nana was practically family. I realized that she and Nana had already decided, and that Nana had either asked for or accepted what they called "the family rate," a below-minimum-wage fee that we doubled. Gertrude could give us three days a week.

But the bridge—the bridge, that would be a problem.

Gertrude almost never drove into Philadelphia from her home in New Jersey because you had to cross the Delaware River on the Ben Franklin or Walt Whitman Bridge. Maybe she could learn, but the thought of it made her awfully nervous. She seemed to shrink down into the passenger seat of our minivan. She looked frightened but determined. Maybe she could get used to it, she said, if she rode back and forth enough to feel as if she knew the route as well as she knew the roads in New Jersey. But getting used to the city: she couldn't tell how long that would take. I felt a tiny, craven impulse that I recognized more often as the gravity of life-and-close-to-death settled into our house and changes to our family's life began to make themselves evident. So how about this: How about I came and got her in the morning and took her home in the evening? We'd do it for a while, and she could tell me when she felt confident enough to try to drive herself?

I had no idea how I'd manage this chauffeuring. Nana had begun to sleep longer in the morning, so maybe I could see Zoë off to school and then get to Jersey and back before Nana awoke. But Nana still did not know the house and sometimes awoke with a start and called out, frightened. So maybe Bob could stay home until we returned. Even with partial deafness, Nana could hear Bob's baritone. His voice, as we learned, comforted her.

So, we began. In less than a month, Gertrude, in her champagne-colored SUV, a surprisingly tall car for such a small woman, came tooling up our driveway. She entered with a happy "Good morning!" no matter Nana's muttered response, opened the shades we installed specially to block the light, and helped Nana to a brief morning toilette. Then she bustled downstairs to cook, with precise care, two eggs over easy, two Jimmy Dean maple-flavored sausages, a slice of buttered raisin toast, a glass of orange juice, and a cup of coffee. Bob named it Nana's Lumberjack Special. Anyone who cared for her had to master it. Eggs hot, coffee dark and sweet, toast crunchy at the crust, buttery and soft in the center. Then, holding the tray, Gertrude settled herself in the electric chair rail we'd installed, flashed the widest of chuckly smiles, and rode up the staircase.

My mother and I had a few terse conversations about the demands of Nana's care and whether she deserved it. Mom resented the time and energy it took. I had less of each week for her and became prickly when she pointed it out. I went so far as to suggest that she tell her girlfriends about her beef with her former mother-in-law.

Within a few months Mom said she'd made peace with the whole situation. "I'm thinking that your children are watching you, and they'll know how to take care of *their* grandmother!"

Chapter 6

At twenty-one, my mother's ambition was to be the best mother ever. When I was born the hospital staff tried to get my mother to bottle-feed me, since that was considered more progressive and sanitary. Like we-know-better Depression-era home economists tried to get people to eat spaghetti with carrots and cream sauce. Mom's body and intuition told her otherwise, and black American experience had taught her that sometimes white science is crazy or aimed against you. So she hedged her bets by nursing, but washing her nipples with alcohol to answer the unsanitary charge, just in case; they cracked and bled. She nursed me for as long as she could stand. She tells how the blood ran into the milk and I nursed as she cried.

Mom determined not to be like her own mother, Nana Hamilton: the often-sick, not-so-practical coloratura church soprano who, Mom said, as a refrain, "could not hold onto a dollar." By the time I was born, Nana Hamilton sang to us in a frayed voice ragged with alcohol and cigarettes: "Oh, Carmidorrrra / Don't spit on the florrrra / Use a cuspidorrrra / That's what it's forrrra!"

Emily Hamilton could be zany! And she might have been more so, had she not been a black woman with three kids and a husband who left her alone with them in Depression-era Harlem while he went to seminary. Quite whimsically, while she was pregnant, Nana Hamilton named my mother after Carole Lombard. The skinny blond actress wore satin gowns and, as far as I could see on TV reruns, barely any underwear, making her the exact opposite of my mother, who came out brown and chunky, and wore—and then confined my sister and me in—extra-rendition girdles and long-line everything. Nothing we had was to jiggle, ever. Period. Mom had no interest in zany blondes or slapstick. What she says about herself as a young woman was this: "The only thing I ever wanted to be was a mother."

Youngest housewife ever, too, surprising door-to-door white salespeople who asked for the lady of the house. She set out to banish her own Harlem childhood traumas: seeing her repossessed living room furniture on the sidewalk in front of a store near 135th and Amsterdam; being responsible too young for wayward, gray-eyed twin sisters who stole her spotlight from the time she was a year and a half; hating the father who abandoned them to attend Wilberforce Seminary, and then returned to drag them from one impoverished AME parish to another.

My mother's first memory of her father is during a Christmas break. He asked her who had sent a Christmas card. She said something sassy. That's the story I remember hearing, although I've attached to it over the years the sense that she may have been just old enough to signify that he did not deserve to know who'd sent the damned card, because he hadn't been there. In any event, it is her first memory of him: he slapped her face.

Mom's ambition was to fix all that. Marrying Nana Jackson's son, my father, Mom's Harry Belafontesque-dreamy high school sweetheart, the week after he graduated from Lincoln University, her twin-sister bridesmaids in coral dresses: that was Step One. Baby, Step Two. Next: He stopped driving a cab and got a job teaching. They bought a little row house in West Philly, new appliances, a funny bug-eyed French car called a Peugeot that Daddy fixed himself. People rolled down their windows at stoplights to ask about it.

I do not know how long they were happy together. As early as I can remember, a leitmotif of tension played through our shiny clean apartment with its thrift-store books and good nutrition. Often anger. Sometimes rage. I loved them so much, and I was afraid of them, individually and together. It felt correct and also very wrong to learn that love and fear was also how I was to feel about God.

Mom says that when I showed temper at six months in the high chair but was just too little to beat—insert low chuckles—she took a pencil and rapped it against my fingers, just a few times, until I got the idea. I was potty-trained, I'm told, soon after my first birthday; reading a few words and writing letters by maybe three; and going to church, dolled up and wearing white gloves that I was not to get "all black and dirty." If that phrase calls up nasty racial slurs, well, that was part of it, yes. Nothing black and dirty, or black and sorry. We were aiming toward uplift, with self-hate beating at our heels like a nightstick.

Meanwhile, however, urban black life required toughness, even fighting sometimes, and one could not shrink from it and make oneself a mark. If kids bullied me in the playground, I was to pick the biggest one, whirl around and knock her down with my book bag.

On television black people stood facing the violence of furious whites and implacable police. The little girls were killed in their church, and I understood that somewhere out there white people in America wished me harm, like the Romans slaughtering innocents to get to Jesus. They collaged in my mind.

In our neighborhood white flight was soaring up and away from West Philadelphia. In school, our teachers preferred white students, and referred to the days before integration as a Paradise Lost, when their *former*—read white—students did this without being asked or reminded, or did that better. We, on the other hand—read black—understood so little that they had to think up new punishments for us, like making boys stand at the back of the room, seven-year-old arms out like crosses till they sagged with fatigue. We girls sat with our backs to them, guilty and precociously protective.

It made sense that as a black child, I could not live in the fantasy world I was liable to fall into at any time. My mother pushed me outside to play with real kids instead of hiding under a table making up stories and being weird. Real kids had their downsides. When a big boy took my book bag at the bus stop, I should not have come home empty-handed and sorry for myself. Did I want a spanking for coming home without the bag my folks had worked for? Or would I go back and get what was mine?

Impossible. The big boy would be long gone. Or worse, he'd be waiting at the stop—and he would kill me. It would be terrible, but at least then my mother would be sorry. They'd have to go to a funeral director, like the ones who advertised on church fans. This thought snagged my vengeful mind: they'd have to buy a short coffin, special made. It would cost more than a regular one, and they were always complaining about expenses, and then, oh boy, they'd really be sorry. They'd cry for the loss of the little girl they'd failed to protect, and, too bad. Too late. This non-Zen meditation on my own death stopped abruptly when the miracle happened. I looked up and there it was: the book bag, tossed into someone's hedges. My heart had been pumping, and now it pumped harder as I stood some feet off looking in a 360-degree circle to check for a trap, and then grabbed the handle of the bag and returned home, a champion.

My childhood continued to deliver more corporal punishment than I felt I could handle, although obviously I'm here on the senior-citizen end of a reasonably sane adulthood, just as obviously I arrived home from the bus stop alive. But I often felt out-of-pocket, out-of-control, sometimes out-of-body. At the first shout of maternal rage, had I been a tiny little comedienne, I would have jumped up onto the stereo console and said into a pretend mic: "Okay, Big Mama: Look, let's just call it for you, okay? What I did—like, I must've lost my damn mind! Listen, listen: that shit will, like, never happen again! Spilling milk, flushing peas down the toilet, playin' doctor under the house with everybody's privates in play . . . I am so over it. No, seriously. *Seriously.*"

But it didn't go like that. The childhood I remember is awash in an internal buzzing, a sort of emotional tinnitus, when things went wrong, or I thought they would. It was fear coming at me from far off, threatening. Sometimes I stood stupidly, because I couldn't think.

—*Do you understand me?*

I said yes, and I wanted to understand, but when I was in trouble, I didn't. I was fogged in, off on a rocky crag, toes gripped, alone. Fifty years later, I accepted an appointment for a year and a half on Philadelphia's Orwellian-named School Reform Commission, and the internal trembling began again. Psychologists from the Institute for Family Professionals who wanted to give classes to teachers on effective, rather than merely punishing, discipline, gave me a report that I read with embarrassed recognition:

> Whenever a child experiences a strong fear reaction, and especially if it is connected to fear of harm and/or abandonment by a parent or caregiver, which includes emotional abandonment, that child will "dump" large quantities of stress and fear hormones into his or her system, which tends to put the child in a state of near panic, meaning he or she is less capable of thinking.

I fastened onto the word "dump." There was not enough money for city children, and I was helping to enforce the inequity. In the large, sunny office I was provided at the school district, people told me appalling experiences of children and families, all of them dumped on and dumping. I felt impotent, like the boy in the first short story I'd ever read all the way through in Spanish. He does bad things, and his hands hang next to him like bells that do not ring.

Not until my grandmother was dead and I tried to look past the last days, back to the luxury of my childhood with her, did I remember my first numinous experience. Even then I could not say it plainly, but instead gave it to a fictional character, a church organist in an opera, who, after a beating, stood in the corner with his pants down and felt, in the notes of music that played in his mind, a gift from God: a cool sense of refreshment to bathe the shame on his buttocks and in his spirit. It's God who promises that boy, as God promised me, that he will not have to hit children when he grows up.

Nana's green carpet was a safe place to replay that blessed assurance, listening to Rachmaninoff over and over, played loudly, until I could hear clearly different instruments playing at once, like conductor Eugene Ormandy and the Philadelphia Orchestra, as if the ability to hear three or four or five sounds at once could bring my outer—or future—world into harmony.

It was accidental meditation, and I called it to mind when I needed it. Which was most of the time, because I was so often so afraid. In our small apartment, I was afraid of my mother's shouting; I was afraid of my parents' anger with each other: screaming arguments that had nowhere to go but to pushing and shoving, like the time they knocked over a lamp and the apartment went dark, and the fury-filled darkness spread from the living room where they slept into the middle room where I slept and then to the kitchen, where we ate together at a red-and-white enamel-top table everything on our plates, period, and looked, for all the world, had you peeked in, like a prosperous young black family in *Jet* magazine.

"The family is a unit," said my father, who told me that at thirteen after his own father left he once attempted suicide.

The unit—and its connections to our varietals of extended family—that was our official internal portrait and aspiration. And in lots of ways, it was true. That's what was so confusing. My parents *were* young and beautiful, each of them enchanting in different ways. He had matinee looks, a wry wit, factual-scientific intelligence, and the tight-jawed inaccessibility of romantic heroes. He required that I find him where he hid, fixing things, napping, or watching one or two favorite shows on TV. She was feisty and funny, naughty, intuitive, pretty, an extrovert and connector, capable of fierceness and needing big, expressive performances of love. Products of divorce, they married to establish a perfect 1950s nuclear family to create the lives they'd inherited only in part. They produced a daughter who was smart and well behaved.

We lived in a two-story, two-apartment row house they'd bought from white people herded by realtors to flee from us. Miss Doris and her family upstairs provided company and rent. Outside our back door was a tiny cement yard. In summertime, after we'd gone inside and my mother had rubbed me down with alcohol to cool me, I sometimes sensed the presence of spirits just outside the screen door, but I did not say so. Later, my maternal great-grandfather's Caribbean folktales confirmed for me that others also experienced spirit presences that lived alongside our African Methodist Episcopal version of Christianity. I did not speak of them. Just like I did not speak of the way I sometimes floated up on the ceiling and watched myself after one of my mother's rages.

American success required a car. My father required it to be special. He bought the Peugeot, with its sunroof that opened with a metallic whoosh that left us open to the sky like herring fillets in a roll-top tin. If someone had taken a picture from above, before my mother lit a cigarette and my father angrily told her not to, we would have looked adorable. How we looked mattered very much to both of them. We did not feel adorable. We did not feel like "a unity," but cold and sometimes hot—warring individuals wishing the others to be different so that we could then be happy.

I assumed that disconnect in elementary school, which perched just at the edge of the University of Pennsylvania and Drexel campuses. We pledged allegiance to the flag and to the Republic for which it stood. I called this nation indivisible. I did not believe it; grown-ups were divided. And when the girls in Birmingham died in the bombing at the beginning of my third-grade year, I understood that the divide was meant for children, too. Liberty and justice did not exist for all, but we pledged it every day, like the unity in our little family.

After the dear love of Mrs. Huggins, the obese kindergarten teacher whose name as well as her body spoke hugs, and Mrs. Hendler with her first-grade professionalism, subsequent schoolteachers seemed to despise us openly. I feared my bus stop, clung to my token and book bag and prayed when big boys walked by. I feared my mother who loved me, but whose maternal ambition and need I felt I could not satisfy. My father withdrew from us both, Mommy and me, if we did not exactly, perfectly match what he needed at any moment. And we seldom did. I feared the 55th Street gang, beautiful young men who sometimes ran through our block and turned on Conestoga, like the pioneer wagons, with fast, thudding rubber-soled feet, wanting to hurt each other. I feared the country to which we pledged allegiance, as it killed Malcolm and Martin, JFK and his brother Robert, and sent young men, like the marvelous Joey up the street, with his almond eyes and black lashes, to Vietnam, which came onto our TV in smoky, fiery scenes of unending and incomprehensible jungle death.

I put the needle onto the black vinyl in my head and played music from Nana's record collection—concertos, opera, spirituals, symphonies—to calm myself. I was to fix my face and stay ladylike, like Nana.

She told a story with happy contentedness about *not working* as a teen when someone came to visit them. Her sister Flora complained about being left alone to make the meal. The older relative, a woman, replied slyly, "Well, Flora, *some*body has to be the lady."

Although my religious-but-not-spiritual grandmother never meant this story to take on biblical overtones, I connected it to the Gospel of Luke where Mary sits at the feet of Jesus while he teaches, and Martha huffs in from the kitchen wanting him to tell Mary to get up and help. Or maybe she just wants Jesus to acknowledge how hard she's working. But he does neither.

"Martha, Martha," Jesus says, "you are worried and upset about many things. But only one thing is necessary. Mary has chosen the better part, and it will not be taken away from her."

In this way, I conflated my grandmother's naughty one-up-ladyship with her sister with a gospel obligation to study and reflection. Being a lady looked a lot like what my mother called being lazy. But it could also mean energetic recreation. Nana let me play the albums over and over, and act out the shows, until I knew each word by heart and could hear each breath. I stepped off the boat as the special confidante to the King of Siam, or hid in the shadows as Tuptim, the enslaved girl who dared perform *Uncle Tom's Cabin* right in front of her masters. Or First Wife, with her brown-butter voice and skin.

From gorgeous First Wife with her painted-on gold dress and bare shoulders, I'd wrap my head and switch to my other favorite contralto, Mother Superior, urging Maria to "climb ev'ry mountain" to escape the Nazis. When it took too long to do the costume changes, I'd lie flat in the sun patch on the floor and try to coax my little-girl soprano lower, pushing the air this way and that to find a deeper tone. It was the sound I loved to feel: a divine female presence, the luxurious mezzo God of delight and strength and forgiveness.

Nearly fifty years later, in my husband's church, swirling in the waves of our organist Roland's musicianship, Nana's head took on its old posture and cast of listening. She relaxed into the sound and the half-dark; and when she reached from her wheelchair and patted my hand, I could take rather than give encouragement. We fell into a side-by-side rest, relieved: she of her failing body, me of my overwork. Each of us, for a moment, not afraid. And having escaped for a moment from ego, we could grieve together for the appalling fact that life was so exquisite, so full of glory and excrement, and, even after a hundred years in the sun, so short.

One night, when he'd finished practicing, Roland asked whether Nana had a favorite hymn he could play for her.

"Did he say something?"

I repeated the question into her ear. She looked up toward him, thought for some moments, and then said, "My *father's* favorite hymn was 'Onward, Christian Soldiers.'"

Roland smiled widely, changed his stops, and played it through, dipping us in the nineteenth-century Salvation Army, *St. Gertrude* tune. It sounded like Churchill and wars and definitely like her father as she'd described him, the colored Victorian papa. Of course he'd like his Christianity warlike, he who knocked their elbows, if they put them onto the dining table, with the knife handle.

Roland built, slowly, the second verse, adding stops until the thickly textured sound pulled us, like an undertow, into its power and grandeur, vibrating through our bodies. It wasn't about real war, though men had used it for that. It was about war with Satan's hosts and hell's foundations, which I'd thought of for years as metaphors for the evil we do, all by our damn selves. But it was becoming clear to me that at 101, with a failing heart, Nana's battle was real and to-the-death; nothing metaphorical about *that*; and the characters who peopled the stories of our faith were visiting her all night long. Maybe that was why she'd gone hard of hearing, as if life's mixing board lowered the volume on today to bring up other voices it was time for her to hear. Not that she was trying to hear anything from death.

Chapter 7

Nana had managed to live in her house until she was ninety-nine years old by engineering work-arounds to age in place: despite strokes, a car accident, and a dose of arthritis medicine that gave her one day of pain-free walking, followed by weakness that put her into the wheelchair. It represented the prosperous family reset for the woman who had divorced her first husband, my grandfather, when my father was thirteen, and raised Dad in small, rented houses in West Philadelphia while she wrote her ex cold, threatening letters about support, storing carbon copies in the safe at her office.

In the mid-1950s Nana married Pop-Pop, whose proper name was Earl Jackson. Having had one wrecked marriage, Nana put strict limits on the second. They shared the same birthday, but not finances. They slept in the same bedroom, but in twin beds that rolled apart so that Nana could tuck the sheets in separately. That's what she told me. And although they also shared nearly forty years in the stucco-and-stone colonial with dark green trim, it felt to me like it was Nana's house that Pop lived in. Nana determined that the wall-to-wall carpeting would be an olive green and the living room walls a matching sage. Pop mowed the lawn, but Nana added one after another spring-flowering tree and shrub; she lined the windowsills with African violets, aloe, and dieffenbachia, which she told me never to eat, because it would give me lockjaw; she chose the andirons and record albums and book-club art books and what I think was an Everett upright piano that she played occasionally when I was very little and taught me notes on. Pop agreed with and deferred to her taste. The house was her brand.

In it Nana and Pop entertained colored social-club people who swept in a few times a year. Nana sometimes referred to them as their "set." They did indeed seem to me like similar people who belonged together, not only because of their light-brown-to-white skin colors, but more so because of the confident music of their voices. In good weather they clumped around the house and patio in mostly separate groups of men and women. They gossiped; they referred to events in the past; they asked about each other's families; they sparred and argued, usually with humor; they played cards, although never with the knuckle-banging fury of my maternal family from New York; they drank beers and mixed drinks and ate Nana's tidy casseroles and asked for recipes.

There were a few "characters," as Nana called them. My favorite was an elegant bronze woman named Mrs. Yancy, whose husband had been a shortstop in the Negro Leagues and later a scout for the New York Yankees and the Phillies. Mrs. Yancy said unexpected things and seemed freer than the other women to speak her mind. When Pop-Pop talked to some of the men about baseball, he'd refer to Campy, Roy Campanella, a catcher who played in the Negro Leagues, then in Mexico, and for ten years, before his car accident, for the Brooklyn Dodgers. Campy was inducted into the Hall of Fame in 1969.

Pop had played with amateur teams, as he called them, but however amateur they were, some money was involved, and he was proud of having been the one to collect it. He'd refer to things and to baseball players by their nicknames, and interrupt to add what he knew. He'd point his finger or touch someone's chest with it and laugh. He'd call me his "Little Rascal," like the old TV show, and sit me on his knee like a prop. He was proud to have stories to tell. He was proud of his green-carpeted home and the casseroles and wife with such good taste in everything. He was proud of his little girl, who was smart as a whip.

I felt a little embarrassed sometimes at Pop's shiny-bright company voice. Years later, when we were alone, he taught me how to throw a ball. Being a pitcher, even if you weren't great, he said, made you useful to the team. Maybe I'd told him how miserable I was in our new school with no friends; maybe he could see it. Certainly, I took his advice and pitched, with obsessive practice and control, in order to get picked onto playground teams. He also told me, as we walked back to the house, that he hadn't really played all that much. He was grinning into the sunshine, but not happily. "Here's the thing," he said, giving me his strategy for inclusion: he'd always had a car, and he could count the money. Some of the guys who were great players didn't have good enough jobs to buy cars. Some of them couldn't read or write so well, or count. Pop had a desk job selling steel and routing trucks to deliver it; he was someone who could talk to team owners and league organizers about money, and pick it up, and count it, and tell white men to their faces when they'd cheated the team.

Pop's parents had come here from Jamaica, white-looking people like himself, both of them. They were amateur actors, he said, although I never knew what they did for money. His mother's maiden name was Ifill. In the days before the Internet, when I first entered the workplace and began to travel, Pop asked me to look up other Ifills, call them and find out their pathway to the States. It was exactly the kind of thing that the son of actors, the extroverted steel salesman, would do, but that I was mostly saved from, since Ifills are so few. (I did, however, tell it to television journalist Gwen Ifill the one time we met; and she grinned at the idea of long-ago Jamaican cousins.)

Pop-Pop loved showy indulgence. He bought the biggest greeting cards in the store for every holiday. When it was time to sell the house, there they were, one after another in a box in the attic: *To My Sweetheart*, over and over again, *Merry Christmas*, *Happy Mother's Day*, *Happy Birthday*: big, swirling italics shedding glitter that had been waiting forty years to reflect off someone's fingers again. He drove me to Green Valley, a place that smelled like cold dairy and sugar, and we'd buy fresh-made ice cream. One time when we went, they were closed unexpectedly, and all night he grumbled about disappointing "the little girl," even after I had happily eaten ice cream from the supermarket.

Pop loved to be special and was hard to embarrass. He

walked to the front of restaurant lines to slip a bill to the host to let his family in first. He liked walking past the other people waiting. And motioning for us to walk ahead of other people, too. I remember slinking, eyes on the floor. He liked to pay for things and protect us.

Pop came to Grammom's funeral. In just a week after she died, no one made supper, hot and salty, ready on the stove to feed and anchor us. Then, in church, at the funeral service, it happened: my great-grandfather Pap Drayton said something like, "Oh, my wife," and toppled off the pew onto the red-carpet church floor. Pop-Pop appeared at the end of our pew with his business suit hustle-bustle. Mom moved me toward him.

"Come on, honey. Pop-Pop's gonna take you outside."

Pop reassured me that my great-grandfather had probably fainted because it was so hot in there, and that he'd be all right. I understood that he was giving me a safe, believable counternarrative to my maternal family, who had screamed together, when Pap Drayton collapsed, that we were now going to lose them both. Pop held my hand tight as we walked outside the church, alongside its rough stone wall. I was crying. Pop bobbled my hand now and then and made funny impatient sounds, *humph*s, because he wanted me to stop.

We were still near the door when a brown-skinned man came out, about Pop's age, and confronted us. He had a proud, angry face, and he spoke to Pop-Pop loudly. I cannot recall the timbre of the voice, only its diction, so practiced that it seemed false. He spoke over my head directly to Pop, asking who he was and where he was taking me. I seem to remember that in this instance, as in so many others when we were out in public together, people assumed that Pop was white, and therefore wondered about our connection. But this almost never happened in black institutions. It seemed especially strange in a church.

Pop held my hand very tightly. "Who are you?"

"I'm the child's grandfather," said the man.

Whoa! I thought, *I don't know you.*

Pop studied the man's face for a moment. It was clear that he understood something I didn't. Then he said with gruff authority: "*I'm* the child's grandfather."

The two grandpas reared back like old sea lions in a TV nature show. They had sparred. Without another word, the other man went back into the church.

Later, it became a story that the adults told and repeated. He was my mother's father, the same man who had slapped Mom's face on his Christmas break from seminary. Later, once he was ordained, he carried his family from one church-mouse-poor parish to the next in the AME First District: from rural Delaware where he'd drowned my mother's dog, who'd started sucking eggs; to parishes where no one could play piano for hymns except Nana Hamilton; to Bermuda, where he bedded at least one female parishioner, and where Nana Hamilton finally left him. Grammom had been his mother-in-law, and he, whom I'd never met, had come to pay his respects.

When my mother's family told the story, they portrayed him as an arrogant buttinsky figure claiming a right he had not earned. Until the repetition of this story, I did not know that Pop-Pop, the grandfather I was raised with, was not related to me by blood. And other people I didn't know were.

Relationships began to float. They were mysteries. Meeting Reverend Hamilton, my mother's father, aka my grandfather, in church, or just outside of it, was appropriate since church was the place for the great mysteries of separation: a God who was always with us, but far away, watching and participating, giving, loving, jealous, all-powerful, all-loving, and yet capable, somehow, even willing to let us stumble and fall and suffer and die. To which our correct response was: Thy will be done.

The story as the grown-ups told it also held a tinge, maybe just a whiff, of mockery of Pop-Pop, too.

"Don't worry, honey," Pop had said to me that day after Surprise Grandfather withdrew back into the church. "Nobody's gonna take my Little Rascal."

After the funeral, I found myself thinking of death, trying to take it in. I studied the professional headshot of Pop-Pop's actress daughter who had died before I was born. The young woman in the photo was achingly, tragic-mulatto beautiful, like a young Rita Moreno. She parted perfect lips I knew must be red from the deep, perfect gray in the photo. This glorious young woman who held blackness and whiteness in her shining black-and-white eyes, had signed the photo to Pop from his "Little Rascal."

The Little Rascals ran episodes on TV sometimes, with high-pitched, urgent voices from other eras and black kids named for breakfast cereals. Pop's name for me, I realized, was not mine; it had been hers, this stunningly gorgeous creature in the photo; and his name for her was not one he had thought up himself, but grabbed from the show. Maybe Pop's indulgence had less to do with me than with her, the original Rascal whose name I dared not ask. She was more beautiful than I'd ever be. And dead, like Grammom. Except this young woman had committed suicide. Now, she was dead and quiet like stones, not dead and alive again, like Jesus. If she were, Pop wouldn't need to keep calling me by her nickname.

Chapter 8

From then on, I knew that I was not Pop's real Little Rascal. I was a relatively unattractive, nappy substitute. That he had decided to call me by his dead daughter's nickname made me feel different about Pop-Pop, although I could not have said how. She, the nameless daughter—no doubt someone told me her name, but throughout childhood I forgot it—she had been too beautiful and too tragic to live. I, who wanted so much to be loved and approved, I recognized the romance of early death. I picked it up from that photo and from *The King and I* and *West Side Story* and my community of black Christians who said of people who died young that they were too good to live. Beautiful, tragic, elegant, dead.

I, on the other hand, seemed to thrive like a green bay tree. It felt like the more vulgar option, greedy, hardscrabble. This despite the times my mother said, with remembered urgency and fear: "You almost died." Seems like I did it more than one should: I almost died when I ate the pills at two years old and the doctor called my aunt who worked at the hospital, because he knew her, and told her to come see me, 'cause maybe it would be the last time; I almost died when my parents rushed me to the hospital with asthma attacks worse than usual and couldn't breathe. I almost died that time a doctor urged: "Stay with me!" and although I wanted to be good and obey, I was just too tired, and let go and thought I would die, but woke up alive. I *thought* I would die the time my tonsil removal went awry, and they had to stitch up my throat inside, and I couldn't have ice cream, and the other kids went home the next day, and when they saw I was sucking my thumb and messing up the stitches, they put a cast on my arm, and I stayed awake all night contemplating trying to suck the other one, because how else could I fall asleep in the dark metallic room. *Do Jesus.* And speaking of Jesus, and almost dying, there were the times when my mother prayed to Jesus saying that if she hit me, she'd kill me, and I felt the rage coming off her skin because I was never good enough. Ever. So I prayed to Jesus, too. And damned if I didn't live, despite making her angrier and angrier, all the time, and her hitting me the times when she did not feel the need to bring Jesus in to help her. Still, death seemed very close to our lives.

We did not talk about death at Nana's house. Nana never shouted to the deity to keep from killing me; she never rushed me, or disapproved, or withdrew from me. But sometimes, when she thought I was farther away than I was, she spoke to Pop-Pop in a voice so sharp and condescending, sometimes even with disgust, that I could not, at first, believe it was her. Nor could I believe that Pop-Pop took it, with a

mumbled response, maybe, or a singular high-pitched protest, and then silence. Sometimes he'd humph and go out for
a while in his car.

The voice she deployed with Pop was similar, but more
personal, and therefore scarier, than the professional hard-
ball voice she used with tenants who came into the office
with what seemed to my child's mind reasonable requests.

Nana referred to the office as The Estate. It was the
Estate of G. Edward Dickerson, a parcel of buildings in
South Philadelphia, that had been bought by G. Edward and
Addie Dickerson, her father Will Hagans's associates in early
twentieth-century racial justice fights. G. Edward Dickerson had graduated from Temple University Law School in
1902, had worked as assistant solicitor for the city, and in
1919 defended several black men charged in riots over scarce
housing. He succeeded in suing the county for damages to
property destroyed by the mob. In addition, he also brought
to trial police officers who killed a black man. She, Addie
Whitehead, was the city's first black female notary public;
co-organizer of the city's YWCA; chair of the National Council of Church Women; representative to the 1924 Prague,
Czechoslovakia, meeting of the Women's International
League for Peace and Freedom; chair of the Foreign Relations Committee of the International Council of Women of
the Darker Races; board member of what was then Bethune-
Cookman College (now University). Nana's father ran the
office after they died.

Their only son died before them, so they willed the buildings they'd bought over their lifetimes to be used to "improve

the Negro race." When Nana's father died, he left Nana as trustee of the parcel.

She worked there four mornings a week, managing the apartments for 6 to 10 percent of the rents. After she cleared the mortgages in the late 1950s, she began awarding scholarships, in accordance with the Dickersons' will, "to aid worthy students in obtaining an education . . . and to assist members of the Negro race whenever their civil and political rights are involved." The rents stayed low, and Nana kept the expenses correspondingly low. Once you clear a loan, she said, never take out another. Never.

The office, originally Dickerson's, felt like the set of a 1930s office drama with a corner storefront. On the rare school holiday, if I'd spent the night, I'd go to the office with Nana in the morning. She'd open the safe, as big as a closet, reminding me never to get my fingers in the way of the five-inch-thick doors. We'd water the thirty-year-old snake plants in the window. If there were a reason to open the closed-up storefront across the hall, she'd let me step in. It was still and stale and dusty. In some places the floorboards had rotted. I could see through to the dirt crawl space underneath. It had been a tailor's shop for years until the tailor died. It became an ice cream store, and finally a candy store Nana suspected of fronting for drugs, so she put out the owner and stopped renting it. Instead she used it for storage, including to save people's furniture for them after evictions. Upstairs and all up and down the street were apartments lived in by people who'd migrated from the Jim Crow South.

Tenants would come in to pay rent or partial rent or beg off for a week; they'd stop in to show off grandchildren or tell good news; they'd complain about problems in the apartments.

"Ms. Jackson, the mice come up from the woman down-stairs, and they're just runnin' all night."

"You keep food out? Any food anywhere, they'll find it."

"How long I been keeping house? You know there's not a speck."

"I can't remember your stove up there . . ."

"Well, it's old, that's for sure. But I clean behind it. What I'm wondering about is an exterminator."

"I don't have money for an exterminator."

"Well, Ms. Jackson, what am I supposed to do? I mean about the mice?

"I don't have money for an exterminator. Maybe you'll have to get a cat."

We'd leave the office in her car, the white Thunderbird with red leather interior, or the light blue Starfire, and drive over the Delaware River to New Jersey for a grilled cheese sandwich before a trip to Cherry Hill Mall or a nice, quiet afternoon at home, me playing with the record player, and her cutting fabric on the dining room table or maybe stitch-ing something in the tiny, east-facing sewing room lined with Book-of-the-Month Club editions.

It was confusing. Nana's suburban house was more expensive and clearly culturally more desirable; it looked like houses on TV, and so did Nana's white neighbors. But

Mrs. Green across the street from the office could—and did—walk downtown in twenty minutes. She'd stop in to say hello carrying a bag from one of the department stores. On short school days, she'd say that she'd taken off work and was about to pick up her girls to hear the Wanamaker organ concert. I wanted to live where you could walk downtown and hear the organ concert and see the Christmas lights every day! I liked the narrow brick houses that sat unashamedly on the sidewalk, with people able to lean out the windows and talk to each other.

But beyond taste, there was the injustice of it. We drove home in Nana's latest late-model car for long, delicious afternoons at home after mornings spent renting apartments Nana would not have wanted to live in. I didn't know how to hold in my mind the two Nanas: she who was so tender with me, and she who was so cold to the people who lived "down to The Estate."

I asked a few times. Nana assured me that "this was *business.*"

Nana and Pop-Pop continued to take me, and then my sister and me, on weekends. We'd likely go somewhere, on an outing, maybe to my favorite, the historic Batsto Village, now a state park, because, as Pop said, "the child loves history." But things had changed.

If there was a presentation, blacksmithing or weaving—those are the ones I remember wanting to return to—Pop-Pop would push me in the back of my shoulder blades to get me right up to the front as he stood there behind me. Now that I was getting older, I resisted moving to the front with him, choosing to stand back with Nana and hold Carole. I knew that Pop would stand up there, taking in the presentation, because we were supposed to come first. It was Pop-Pop's version of W. E. B. Du Bois's explanation in *The Souls of Black Folk* of how he came to want to beat the white children in any contest.

I also began to inspect Pop's collection of paperbacks that Nana called trash and did not get into the house proper—not on her sewing room shelves or in the den where we watched television, but lined the stone ledge in the sun parlor, where he read them fast, sitting on the porch furniture, with his thumbnail between his teeth. In middle school I picked one up and found myself up to my mental short-hairs in a sex scene such as the old, blurry sex-education movies could never, ever have pointed toward. Whoa! I did not like the characters or what they were doing. But I couldn't stop reading. One damned thing led to another. Oh my goodness, and I found myself flushed and warm and damp. I wondered how he read these things, one after another, sitting there chewing his thumb, and giving no indication at all of what they were picturing.

Chapter 9

When Pop-Pop died, Bob and I drove to Nana's house to stay with her until the undertaker came. Just a few people seemed to fill the house with a synthetic condolence as they brought in gear and then carried Pop's body from the den, down the stairs, and out the door in what looked like a gray corduroy envelope. Only toddler Zoë jabbered normally. At ten, Laura looked back and forth tearfully as if for some way to escape.

Within a month or so, Nana learned that Pop had left her with unexpected debt. How? He'd worked fifty years for Morris Steel Company, giving himself a tagline that I still cannot believe I'm remembering correctly—*Never late; one day absent.* The only reason he missed was that his car refused to plow through the streets on one of those snowpocalypse days when elected officials begged nonessential workers to stay off the roads. When Pop retired from Morris, he received stock earnings. Nana and he went on cruises; they painted the house and bought newer cars.

A few days after retiring, Pop got himself hired at a tiny steel company whose office sat on the banks of the Schuylkill

River, across from a city dump site, at the foot of a bridge still named for the eighteenth-century ferry once operated there by George Gray. On the other side of the bridge was a baseball field where Pop and his amateur black teams had played. He sold steel to contractors and routed the truckers, like a pre-GPS calculator, studying maps, discussing what highways they should take and determining how long they could drive safely in order to get the load to the buyer on schedule. Pop told me that his mostly black drivers trusted him not to create dangerously long days or impossible routes to avoid a dollar in tolls; they were real men to him, not objects. His white bosses liked that he could find out the real deal from guys "out back."

Then, having worked fifteen years at the second company, Pop-Pop retired again, and this time took up a part-time job at the Philadelphia airport selling seats on vans that went through South Jersey to Atlantic City casinos. He still glanced at his watch every half hour or so when he was home, as he had for more than fifty years, to check schedules in his head.

So, Pop always worked; always made money, and lived as large as he could, but, we thought, within his means. Then, in his early nineties, he suffered a stroke while preparing his taxes. His credit card bills began coming in. Now Nana found out about their debt. She let me know that she had reason to believe he'd kept a woman on the side. His retirement nest egg: all gone.

Besides his personal credit card debt, for which Nana was liable, and which she paid, there was some other family business. I heard about it sideways, just as I had learned important information as a child: it seemed that Pop had "held" some money for my father and spent that, too. That seemed to explain why during Pop's final illness my father stopped visiting his room or helping with his care. He began to refer to him by his first name, Earl, rather than Pop.

When I pushed Nana to let me help her organize a memorial service, she told me that she'd taken care of Pop after his stroke because that was what one human being does for another, and that she paid the undertaker because it was the right thing to do. But she refused to go to the expense of a funeral. She did not bother to pick up his ashes. Maybe, she suggested, if I was so worried about it, I could scatter his ashes behind first base at the black baseball field by Gray's Ferry Bridge. When I told her that I thought the city had laws about disposal of human remains in children's playgrounds, she humphed.

So I brought Pop's ashes to our house. What I really wanted was some altar-like nook, tucked away from where the children might get to it. I forget where it started, but pretty soon, it moved to what we euphemistically call the basement. It's a cellar, with roughcast walls, a cement floor, and the usual vintage Philadelphia oil tank, furnace, and hot-water heater. Plus, a washer-dryer set that the store delivers for installation in pieces because row house doors are too narrow to bring them in whole. The sturdy brown cardboard box of ashes squatted wherever I found space—and then moved around. After a rush to grab beach chairs and the umbrella or to put away Christmas decorations, it might get shoved out of sight.

"Have you seen the box?"

"What box?"

"From the undertakers."

"Undertakers?"

"Pop-Pop!"

"I don't know. Haven't seen it for a while. Do we still have it?"

Each time the dusty little box disappeared I imagined that somehow it had fallen behind a shelf and burst open. In my mind's eye, I'd see ashes and gritty bits of bone spilling out of the heavy-duty Ziploc bag, mixed into the brick dust where the wall met the floor, heaped onto a dried-up mouse carcass or into the pressure cooker. I'd never experienced a relative's death so unremarked. It was a Greek tragedy robbed of its import, and I was not Antigone, but just a stand-in L'il Rascal. I wasn't looking for my grandfather's bones, I was ignoring them. I wanted to wish him peace, and to give my children a spiritual marker, a time and place to acknowledge Pop-Pop's life.

Nana wasn't trying to hear it.

My sister felt the same way I did. So, many months later, Carole and I organized a tiny memorial service. We split the costs of a modest columbarium space and an urn. Because Nana and Pop did not attend a church, the priest at our Episcopal Church of the Advocate agreed to officiate. No leaflet or obituary, just the comfort of words and ritual. To our tiny group huddled in one side of the transept, Carole gave a moving remembrance about Pop playing baseball and teaching her to keep going. Nana and my father sat through it stone-faced. Our priest said the sacramental words, and

Carole and I went to the graveyard together to deposit Pop's remains.

About that time came the call. An older woman called the house, Nana said, asking for Pop. Nana said that her voice sounded timid. Suspecting this woman to be the recipient of the money she was then paying back to the credit card companies, Nana answered curtly that Pop was not home, but refused to give the caller the satisfaction of confirming that he was dead.

Years before, when my first husband and I divorced after just a few years of marriage, Nana complimented me on my good sense to end it early, before children. Then she told me this story, one that she repeated when she came to live with us in the rectory: her first husband, my father's father, would not teach her to drive an automobile, accent on the third syllable. This was during the Depression. Their parents had been among the hundred-thousand-plus African Americans who had rolled up on Philadelphia in the Great Migration, doubling their representation from 5.5 percent of the city's population in 1910 to 11 percent by 1930. Nana's husband was the son of Jamaican immigrants.

Somehow, in Prohibition-era Philadelphia, with its speakeasies and organized crime, just five years after a politician's short-lived reform *removed roofs from squad cars* to keep cops from sleeping in them, and back when the ward leader and City Council members were required to okay each and every appointment in their districts, somehow this good-looking young black man and a few dozen others managed to get onto the police force.

Well, when he told her he wouldn't teach her, that she was just a woman who couldn't learn, etc., she made up her mind what to do. Without telling him, my grandmother applied for a learner's permit. Over time—months, maybe a year, she couldn't remember, it had been so long ago—she practiced on her father's car. Will Hagans had had a car during the era of the dusters and took his family for Sunday drives during Nana's childhood in Philadelphia. Records show that in 1921, he paid a settlement of $750 to a blind woman who had been struck "by his vehicle" as she was being led across the street. That would have been a dozen years before Nana's stealth driving lessons. Maybe she didn't even know about it. She passed her own test on the first try. And when the Pennsylvania Bureau of Highway Patrol issued her a license, she hid it in the drawer underneath her brassieres, where it gave her a delicious thrill of power.

Just as you don't tell your daughters about your own menstrual history—the fibroids and blocked ovaries, the miscarriages and bleeding—until they've passed puberty, Nana didn't tell me this story until I was divorced, as she had been before she remarried, as my grandparents on my mother's side had been, and my parents, and my aunts: virtually everyone between our generation and our great-grandparents'. But by the time she did tell me, Nana expected that my life experience now qualified me to enjoy the ruse. It was a delicacy of resentment. Just think—here she couldn't help but start to chuckle—him going on so high and mighty, giving her rides here and there, picking her up, asking whether she had car fare for the trolleys. And her going along with it, just as nice . . . *Hah!*

Sitting in the suburban New Jersey kitchen where we'd eaten and cooked all my life, I sensed the specter of this naughty Nana peeking in from the past at the back screen door. It had been my childhood metaphor for a porous threshold between my conscious mind and a wordless and mysterious apprehension of an unseen community nearby, but separate. She felt like the old, black-and-white photos of herself, hair bobbed or pulled back, usually ladylike, sometimes sly and sultry in wool bathing suits on the beach in Ocean City. Soon she would write those angry letters about late child support. She was the woman who wanted cash on hand at all times, cash being an answer to blackness and womanhood and other inescapable marks of inferior status. The young woman who peered out of this story sucked her teeth at me. After all, she'd been the girl, head shaven and quarantined for scarlet fever, who'd eaten every single shiny Temple orange—hers *and* her little brother's before he got them.

"You opened that drawer every day and just knew it was there, *huh*?"

"Yup!" My grandmother almost never said yup, except for comic effect, like 1920s songwriters used "ain't." Now she said it and spread a satisfied, Cheshire-cat grin over her usually poised face.

Sometime later, when Nana and her first husband, the police officer, were arguing, in order to show his superiority, he referred to the fact that *she couldn't even drive.* She'd been waiting for that. Upstairs she bounded, right to her bureau drawer, and "pulled out the license."

Here, when she told the story, she held her right hand aloft, thumb squeezed against index and third fingers, as if the card were right between; as if her large-knuckled fingers, shaped like mine, but whiter and thinner, had clutched the memory of resentment until it had burned away all the flesh.

Then she let go the low hollowed-out dry-paper laugh: *Hah! She showed him!*

She'd look at me for the reaction shot. Motes in the air bobbed around her, freshly amused at each telling. I wanted to say to her, like a friend of my daughter's used to say, shaking his head, eyes on the ground: "What can I say? I got nothin'."

Theoretically, the image of her twenty-something self, spunky, capable, refusing to be bullied, that should have spoken to me. But when I reached for my sense of humor, or even dutiful loyalty, I found that they'd snuck down to the basement together to hide behind the knotty-pine bar my dad had built her, back when he called her "m'mother," as in "I'd do anything for m'mother"; back before they'd stopped speaking to each other for seven years, when everything was supposed to be fine, and I was fool enough to think it was.

Eyebrows raised, she'd invite me into the bitterness that passed for maturity: *Grow up. The emperor was always naked. There's nothing you can trust except cash in a shoe box. Get it? Laugh with me!*

Instead, I wanted to get into my own car and drive away to Naïve Land, where God has placed eternity in the human heart, just as it says in Ecclesiastes, and where each of us can hear music in the air: "Yes, God is real," Mahalia sings. "He's real, for I can feel him in my soul."

After she was taken off the hospice list, the exhilaration of beating death began to sag into the continued hard task of living impaired. Nana's eyesight was lousy; she could only hear most voices through the earphones connected to the microphone; she got around by wheelchair, transferring from bed to chair, and gathering all her strength to rock-climb down three steps to the landing where the chair rail waited. Now, when she was unoccupied, Nana began to vent her rage at all the losses. Now and then, she would sit on the side of the bed, pound her fists, and ask, "Why am I still alive?"

I would answer that maybe God wanted her to have an intimate relationship with someone who would tell her no.

She didn't laugh at that any more than I laughed at her secret driver's license.

Chapter 10

As I search for ways to tell how it felt to have Nana in the house—yep, I do mean that as a reference to Elvis in the house, or Tupac in the house, or some other dead celebrity who leaves afterglow energy—as I try to describe her presence, the metaphors I find seem to require water: a shallow fog had rolled in; or, better yet, a frozen ice crystal appeared in the landing that caught the light in new ways and made me shiver.

That tracks better with my dreams of winter, as if I were snowed in unexpectedly, like when Pop-Pop forgot my boots and I had to wear Nana's too-big galoshes to go out and play on the porch. But unlike those days, when Nana would fix things, now it was my porch, and death was on the horizon, and I couldn't fix that. Nana did not want to know. Her body knew, however, and like animals sharing a den, our bodies, too, felt it.

While we slept fitfully, New Year's slunk in. Nana made it to her hundred-and-first year. Then Epiphany, when maybe I made the Three Kings cake or maybe not. Again with the Herod. Again with the Wise Men, and the boys in Sunday school jostling each other to choose which of the Wise Men/kings' crowns and jeweled vests each one would fit this year; and the little children clamoring to huff the complex frankincense and bitter myrrh from the painted wooden boxes where I kept them on the Christmas shelves in Ziploc bags to slow down the dust. And the stories and songs, and then John the Baptist in the wilderness waiting for the One, finding him, baptizing him.

One of our Sunday school boys, Jake, drew a dove that year and wrote: "This is my beloved son. Listen to him."

I put it on the mirror in the hallway to remind me to listen to the children. I wished I could listen more deeply to Jake and the others and my own children, but I felt as if Nana's presence registered so loudly that I kept turning down the volume.

Sometime in that first January, the muscles in my shoulders and upper back froze up. It was as if someone had turned a knob and it got stuck there, twisted. I described it as the body's equivalent of when our old push-button Dodge Dart station wagon just seized. Later, an acupuncturist, a masseuse, and my many alternative medicine body-mind books claimed that the places that clamped shut are those that make it their business to protect the heart and lungs. Like many protectors, they can go to hypervigilance and get stuck there.

I began a new semester of teaching at the University of Pennsylvania, and spoke firmly to myself about welcoming the new writing students and finding ways to be curious about them and their work. Then, at church, came the video conference from Trinity Church Wall Street on religion and violence. Oh, Lord. Months before I had encouraged Bob to participate as a satellite spot, the only one in our region, saying that I'd be happy to provide the necessary light catering: a continental breakfast and simple lunch. He said yes.

Now, it seemed impossible. I could not breathe in without discomfort. I could barely lift a pan and certainly not a tray full of fruit, cornbread, boiled eggs, and such.

So I hired out. I'd recently contracted with a housekeeping service to clean the rectory every other week. Now, I hired my daughter's friend, who had recently lost her job and needed work. She did the day-and-a-half light catering of breakfast, midmorning drinks, and lunch for twenty participants. I greeted people and smiled as our young helper moved with brisk, but friendly, competence through the first wave of food and service. Then, I drove to work thinking about how unforgiving Nana was about illness and weakness, and wishing that I could dissolve the hard, sharp pain in my shoulders by finding in myself compassion toward my own muscles.

Perhaps the body is saying what the mind will not acknowledge. What is your body saying to you?

One of the websites I read asked this infuriating question. All I could think of was a course I'd taken that interpreted elements of what was then called Ebonics. Skipped words, some researcher wrote, advanced the economy of American English. Added phrases, on the other hand, which might seem redundant or unnecessary, indicated emphasis despite indirection. When my green-and-crunchy rehab sites talked about pain as a way for the body to say something the mind wouldn't let itself know, a voice inside kept editing what I read into a black directive: *Say it out your mouth*.

But I couldn't.

Chapter 11

As she got stronger, Nana demanded to help with dinner. *Oh, honey! Give me something to do.*

I resisted. The first thirty minutes of dinner had been my own time, the introvert just home from an extrovert work life. I rested between work and family with familiar actions: washing, cutting, sometimes with the radio news. During the second half of cooking, my daughters and husband would join in, each one taking on accustomed tasks, speaking little—"Water? Seltzer? Spoons tonight? Tablespoons?"— easy and regular. Breathe, smile. Dinner prep as group yoga practice.

Nana loved to watch, now that she was part of this family. She wondered at how we never ran into each other, and how Bob "fit right in." But she wouldn't just sit like a lump. If she was going to live here, she would help. She'd string beans, break apart florets of broccoli, shell limas. With a knife that wasn't so sharp as to cut her, but not so dull as to tax her strength, she could still peel apples and potatoes, mostly by feel. So, besides other criteria, our menus now had to include each night some food whose preparation she could help with, that would take her about twenty minutes, and would then cook quickly, before she got too hungry. She needed a bowl to wash her hands in, then a towel to dry them, before and after preparation, and when she asked a question, we had to prop her microphone so that I could cook and talk into it.

We developed similar disciplines in other areas of family life. I grabbed from Bob's sermons little taglines to keep myself from feeling as if I had brought in someone who was taking over our lives. One was the title of a Richard Wilbur poem Bob used a couple of times in sermons, "Love Calls Us to the Things of This World." The commentaries say it's Saint Augustine's lusty answer to First Letter of John's either-or advice to "love not the world, neither the things that are in the world."

Bob used the poem to bring parishioners back to now, on earth as it is in heaven, and I heard his voice talking about fresh linen on the line and a difficult day ahead whenever my mind pulled down from its shelf the poem's revelation that "The soul descends once more in bitter love / To accept the waking body . . ."

Once a week, she and I took a drive, often to the supermarket, often Whole Foods, where I'd push the wheelchair with one hand and pull a cart with the other. When we passed particularly fragrant produce, I'd choose a ripe one and hand it to her to smell before putting it into the cart. Sight and sound had dimmed, but she could still smell and taste. When I saw an especially expensive item, I'd announce it into her microphone—a quarter pound of fancy mush-

LORENE CARY

rooms for *five dollars*—so that she could exclaim with satisfied indignation: *"Whaaaaat?"*

At the register, she'd offer me money from the cash I had gotten her that week and put it into the pocketbook I carried as we shopped.

"Oh, Lord, where's my purse?"

"Right here."

She'd take out the money and look for the denomination. We'd haggle quietly about how much she should contribute, handing the money back and forth, repeating things. People at other registers who could not see her in the wheelchair stared at me as I spoke into a microphone. People behind us showed me their amusement or camaraderie or impatience.

And so, Nana arrested her flight from this world to the next, and established a holding pattern, an orbit around earthly life, in constant contact with mission control. Also snacks.

Some nights as I fell asleep, I was sure that her trying to turn off the TV with the cell phone was actually a ploy, and that she had altered the remote to suck life-force energy from me. I felt infantile, superstitious, and yet so terrified that our relationship was taking me down that I couldn't even tell my husband. On the mornings after this particular fantasy had skittered into sleep with me, some new physical symptom would appear: a muscle knot, a new cyst under my shoulder blade—it's still there—a cut in my eye. I felt like one of Freud's hysterical subjects, minus the sex.

I refused, however, to live with Nana's old-school No Plan B. Hospice was gone, and we needed medical advice.

Three geriatric practices in our area advertised doctors and nurse practitioners who made house calls. I chatted with their receptionists and planned the campaign to get Nana to accept "another stranger coming in here." We'd already talked about the visiting doctor. I gave Nana what I hoped was a fun digest of the doctor's bio, as if we knew her, and then referred back to the time when house calls were standard. Nana liked that. We'd had two conversations. And because there was no way in hell to get information from her old doctor online, I had driven to his New Jersey office so I could report to her that I knew for sure he was not coming back.

The next step was to make the appointment in the room with her, holding her microphone near the speakerphone, so she could hear what we were saying, add her own thoughts, and therefore buy into the process. But before that could happen, on a day when I was driving to Washington, DC, with two women from our organizational partners, the helper who had come to us as catering help called and left a voice message on my cell. Nana had diarrhea, had had an accident and gotten very upset, and she kept asking when I'd be home. By the time we parked in DC and I could ring back on the old cell phones as big as a *Get Smart* shoe phone, the helper had cleaned everything up, gotten Nana to drink a little something, and settled her back in bed. Fresh linen, like Wilbur's poem. I said I'd wouldn't be back until bedtime, but I'd bring ginger ale, crackers, and Imodium if no one else got them before I returned.

In DC, we attended Ysaÿe Barnwell's vocal workshop, which we wanted her to bring to Art Sanctuary, the black arts organization I'd founded in Philadelphia in 1998. The vocalist, composer, and musical director who cofounded Sweet Honey in the Rock stood in a wide room, directing a hundred and fifty people to sing in harmony, sometimes complicated, or close harmony, notes as tight up against each other as lovers. Barnwell sang bass and tenor with the men, and soprano and alto with the women. She was composer and director at once; her voice could do anything. The vibrations ran through my body, working their way into places I'd closed off and forgotten. Singing made me breathe deep into my belly. The ice crystals melted into tears, and I knew how afraid I was that Nana's last bit of life would eclipse my own, that her need would take me away from paying attention to my daughters and husband, and from writing. At the same time I was afraid that our job, my job that they'd been dragged into, was to help her find her way to a good death, whatever that meant, and that I was failing to help her find her way toward it. Instead of walk toward the light, I had gotten the coordinates wrong, and haplessly shouted into her microphone, wheel toward the stairs, or into the closet. But how the hell did I know where the light was for her?

The singing reminded me, in my body, not my mind, of what I believed, but could not always remember: that my grandmother's lifetime habit of isolation could not separate us from each other. Only my fear could do that.

It took three days for Nana to recover her equilibrium. During that time, I made an appointment with the visiting doctor only to have her receptionist call back to cancel. Sorry, but Medicare would not cover the visit. And without proper insurance coverage, the doctor could not come out.

I asked whether I could I pay in cash, just to have her seen while we straightened out this other thing.

No, she explained, because, what if the doctor saw that the medical care required many repeat visits, say, more than we had cash for—not us, but, like somebody?

But how is it, I asked, that for months we've had hospice coverage? Well, right there, the young woman said, that was a clue. I should call Holy Redeemer to see how they did it. Catholic hospitals, she whispered, *they* knew how to work The System.

The finance lady at Holy Redeemer told me that it wasn't a cunning Catholic subterfuge, but the simple fact that hospice, like hospitals, was paid through Medicare Part A, and Nana's trouble was with Part B, which covered doctors.

Why hadn't the people at Medicare told me that as clearly as she did? I wondered aloud.

Ominously, she answered: "They take a lot of calls in a day."

Medicare reps did tell me that an outstanding doctor's bill was the problem, but I wasn't authorized to receive more specific information. I thought this had to do with the power of attorney form that let me talk to Social Security, but not to Medicare. Whether this was one that required taking Nana to a notary public, I can't recall. There were several of those, in all weathers, and you have to call and see how many steps it takes to get into the office, and whether the place was big enough to fit a wheelchair. It would have been easier if I could have asked, Is this a hole-in-the-wall or a proper office?, but you couldn't. Within a week or two, however, I could talk to Medicare without getting Nana on the phone to give permission.

They still could not give me the information. I waited a day and called back—Tuesday, Wednesday, and Thursday mornings were best, between eight and eight-thirty—hoping to catch someone who'd say different. By now, Nana was better, her immune system having emerged like an ancient Jedi knight summoned by the resistance.

Then I reached José. He had a beautiful Spanish accent, strong enough that I had to listen very carefully and ask him to repeat some things. But he was new to the job, very interested in the service part of customer service, and besides, he was "the kind of guy who likes to get to the bottom of things."

It was José who told me, although he said he probably was not supposed to, that a new company had taken over collecting long-standing bills, which I could understand cost Medicare millions of dollars a year.

I could absolutely understand it!

But how much was the problem on Nana's account? How much was owed?

The number, he said, looked like less than four hundred dollars.

Four hundred dollars? Tears of relief pricked my eyelids. "How can I pay it?"

"Well, this is the hard part. You can't." José said that this looked like it had to do with a car insurance company. Had she had a car accident maybe four or five years ago?

Four or five years before, yes, leaving work, the car had

"gotten away from her," she had said, going faster and faster as she stomped on the brake. She'd never hear otherwise, that maybe she'd hit the gas.

Somehow the car zoomed through the wide intersection at Broad Street without hitting anyone before it bashed into bollards cemented into the sidewalk to protect the pumps at a corner gas station. On her way home from school our older daughter had seen the car.

"Oh, my, God! It looked like Nana's car, but I couldn't believe it! Mommy, you should have seen it. The windshield had a big dent in it from the driver's head. Nana's head!"

That afternoon in the ER, I'd asked Nana, as the resident sewed back on her bottom lip, whether she'd been wearing her seat belt.

Her answer, spoken through her teeth: "It wouldn't have made any difference."

Yes, I told José. There had been a car accident.

Well, it looked like the insurance company had paid bills, yes, but between Medicare and the insurance company was a disputed four-hundred-dollar doctor's fee.

So, I asked him, trying to understand: this was a dispute between the insurance company and Medicare?

Yes, José explained to me. And if I could get *the company* to pay the bill to the doctor—*or* if they would fax a special form that, according to them, this money was no longer owed—then Medicare could clear the account, and we could get her doctor covered.

Okay. I repeated—knowing that I'd never get to talk to José again, that, as in *The Sound of Music*, officials might be waiting offstage even now to take him to the front—not until the insurance company filed a certain form to "zero-out" the dispute could the account be activated. It was important to get the verbs right. Otherwise you could talk to the next person until they hung up on you, because they didn't know that by saying "clear the balance," your poor, ignorant self meant "zero-out."

Although it made me crazy, I never begrudged Medicare its bureaucracy. My commitment to the federal government's attempts to do right goes deep. I was a kid watching on TV as Southern state legislators refused black people the rights of citizenship. Who else could we appeal to but the federal government?

Early on someone had bought me a wrinkly facsimile of the Constitution. I remember loving to read the Preamble. Like the *Book of Common Prayer*, its waves of archaic language washed through the centuries, bringing hope of moral codes that grown-ups failed to live up to, but were never to stop trying. I loved knowing a few of the long words; I loved the capitalization: "a more perfect Union," "domestic Tranquility," "Blessings of Liberty."

So, after my conversation with José, bless him, I talked firmly to myself about millions of four-hundred-dollar bits, and the need for revenue to keep the system going, a system that worked, even for people like my grandmother, a black, Jim Crow-era Republican who'd said for years that the gov'mint had no business in her business.

Then, I began a relationship with Nana's car insurance company, for a car she no longer owned, to clear up an accident she'd had four or five years before, when she was still driving herself to work four mornings a week. I chatted them up about how long she'd insured with them and never had an accident, about her old white Thunderbird with the red upholstery. I told them that her house was still insured with their home insurance. I was craven, like people in kidnapping movies trying to connect with their captors. One woman popped gum in my ear: *I've always loved chewing gum. Funny, eh? That you chew gum, too? Like, what are the odds?*

Customer reps said that they could not accept four hundred dollars from us.

Could they tell me the doctor who was owed, and I'd find that person, and pay him or her, and send them a receipt?

No, sorry, but they couldn't divulge that information.

Whenever they said "information," my hand let go of the string that kept me grounded. Untethered, my mind and I floated out the window. Was it the guy who sewed her lip back on? I could find him, I bet.

I imagined myself standing outside the ER on 10th Street, stalking the doctors at shift change. Fantasies float on the wind and the mind snatches them. They distract you while you talk, which is bad. I no longer understood what the woman was saying in her condescending voice, so I requested a supervisor. The supervisor took a long time to come on the line. By then, I'd written a brief narrative to keep myself on script. I spoke it to her low-and-slow, clean and articulate. It's the telephone voice my children mimic, and then fall out laughing. She said that she was happy to consider it and get back to me.

She did indeed ring back, but she, too, was sorry-but.

Because her voice had sounded competent and compassionate, because she'd had the decency to call back, my eyes welled up. I told her that I was nearly fifty years old, that I ran an urban nonprofit arts organization, that I raised money and supported my staff, that I'd never missed payroll, but that this process—this thing here—had me blubbering on the phone like a baby. For lack of four hundred dollars my grandmother could not access the Medicare she'd paid into since Medicare had been created. Nineteen sixty-five. That had been a big year for me. Nobody on these phone calls had been born yet, but I turned nine that year. It was a coming-of-age year: my baby sister learned to walk; black people finally got the right to vote for real in America. Malcolm was assassinated. With Operation Rolling Thunder we began massive bombing of North Vietnam. Watts exploded after a bad traffic stop. Nana still came to pick me up from school on Friday afternoons, and the olive-green-carpeted house looked and smelled like Sabbath.

No longer. Grandmother could lie here in my house and shit her brains out—that's what had almost happened—and I could take morning after morning off from work so that people far away with no last names could talk to me as if she were a welsher and I were an idiot or a thief.

Now I was bawling. All of it tumbled out: how I had to bring her to live with us, because on the one night I did *not* spend in the hospital, someone pulled out her call-button wire, so that she pushed it and pushed it, but no one could hear.

"She can be difficult," I said, reminding myself why she could not be housed in an institution.

Across the hall, behind me, in her long, sunny bed-sit parlor, Nana now sat on the edge of her bed, long legs swung over the side, thighs cellulite-free, earphones on, eating her Lumberjack Breakfast, and cracking wise with our young helper.

All better!

But what about next time?

Chapter 12

The supervisor said that she was so sorry.

We were silent for a beat. Then she said that in this one particular case she could see no harm in zeroing out the years-old claim and sending the necessary form to release the hold on Nana's Medicare account.

No buts.

There were more steps—paperwork and faxing that had to happen between their different offices. We had a long go-round about the four-hundred-dollar check I offered to send, specifically, whether she could accept it from us when their records showed it owed from the other insurance company. What I remember now are Kafkaesque arguments she ran through aloud about which bureaucratic principles to sacrifice.

In any event, I had to mail signed paperwork to her office, and they'd do something with it for a week, and then she'd have it sent along with a report to their headquarters in another city. Each step would take seven to ten days. She'd call to leave me a message when the company had officially sent to Medicare the official good-to-go form. Then we'd be . . . good to go! None of this could be done by email, then. One transaction could be faxed, but the other had to be mailed through the US Postal Service. The whole thing should have taken two to three weeks. Like the flu.

Except it didn't, because something went wrong, someone didn't get something, and I had to check back with my fave supervisor and then their main headquarters to jump-start the anchor leg of the relay.

A representative at the headquarters talked to me, did not like the sound of it, would not take the baton, and instead started to crawl backwards through the story, repeating my phrases with a snarl in her voice. She was going to undo our arrangement, just for funsies. I reminded her that I was not a complainant trying to get over, but a current customer: Nana wouldn't sell her house, so we still used their company for home insurance.

Oh! She dropped her professional voice for a moment before recovering her Just-say-no stance, and reminding me that the home and auto insurance segments of the company worked independently.

I needed to talk to a supervisor, I told her.

She needed to put me on hold. Aka time out. Aka punishment.

My patient computer waited in front of me with their company's website open to the page listing their leadership, in case I needed to name some names—and then this other idea occurred to me. I had mailed the form to that very office and kept a copy. I typed the address into 2007 Google Earth. There it was: the building in which worked the people who stood between Nana and a doctor. I found myself fixated on the front door. Switching the time-out-stupid-earworm-faux-classical-music hold line to speakerphone, I scoured the USAir website, which had flights out of Philadelphia every few minutes. *Bingo!*

By the time she came on, to tell me that her supervisor was not available, I told her that I was looking at her building, the one with the faux Grecian columns; and that while she was busy *not* getting the supervisor, I had reserved a seat on a flight that would get me there by 3:30 p.m. She could find a supervisor now or, hey, wait until 3:30 for me to arrive in their lobby. Then she could explain that it was *because of her* that this black woman had flown in and popped the hell off. Because I was very likely, at that point, to lose my self-control. Her choice. But why, I asked, would you die in this ditch? Why was it worth her job to ensure that a 100-year-old black lady, my grandmother, who had paid premiums from before you were born and would be paying them after she was fired, could not be seen by a doctor?

I told her again what their building looked like. I growled about my surplus of frequent flyer miles, and how I had the ticket ordered, but could cancel within twenty-four hours. Quoting our young helper, I said that Nana had almost died. And repeated the airline and number of the flight I'd reserved.

Ended up, this latest young woman, though rude and dismissive, was not a total fool. Nana got her clearance.

Chapter 13

"You almost died. Oh, my God, here we are, and you could've died!"

Our helper reminisced with the indestructible Nana about her most recent nearly fatal event, and I could hear Nana notching her belt with another near miss. And despite her occasional "Why am I still here?" tantrums, Nana was not changing her orientation to death.

Only in church, after Sunday school, when we brought the children in for communion, did this come to me. Before church, I opened the blinds, gave her breakfast, and set her up with her TV program. Once the lesson was finished, seeds sprouted, cotton glued onto sheep, stories read, the children and our young Sunday school co-teacher and I, sometimes with toddlers on our hips, fluttered into the service and then spread out in the first pews. The children knew the simple dialogue, and said it in a spoken-soprano choir, happy to have or to be acquiring mastery over the ritual:

Celebrant   The Lord be with you.
    People   *And also with you.*

Celebrant	Lift up your hearts.
People	*We lift them to the Lord.*
Celebrant	Let us give thanks to the Lord our God.
People	*It is right to give God thanks and praise.*

Then, when the *Book of Common Prayer* instructs the celebrant to face the Holy Table and proceed, I'd feel the words and movements and practices pile up: the children getting into position to pass the next eight to ten minutes paying attention or distracting themselves, and my husband's voice occupying the place for celebrant: "It is right, and a good and joyful thing, always and everywhere to give thanks to you, Father Almighty, Creator of heaven and earth."

And then, week after week, it'd be death-prep showtime. *Eucharist* means to give thanks, and the Last Supper is, in fact, last for a reason. Reverend David Bateman, in his version of an explanation of liturgy known as "Instructed Eucharist," reminds us that the simple fourfold pattern used by Jesus to feed the multitudes is reenacted when he feeds his disciples and is picked up in the church's two-thousand-year ritual: "First he *took* the bread. Then he *gave thanks* over the bread. He *broke* the bread, and finally he *gave* it to the people."

So, so simple that it seems almost like worship-cheating to point it out. Bateman calls it "the drama of communion, [when] together we remember what happened in such a vivid way that this memory is brought right back into the present moment."

It's a fraught present moment for me, when Jesus knows death is coming, and Judas will betray him, and Peter will deny him. Fears are ever arising, my Buddhist friend used to say, and Eucharist can sure enough give them space to rise up.

But Nana was *not* readying herself. The heroism of triumphing over death—*Hah! Still here!*—she could not help but enjoy with a slightly congested chuckle. But this Nanatude no longer served her current challenges. Underneath her pride ran a current of anxiety. And when I relaxed into the complicated present moment of Eucharist, with the children drawing or asking for candy, or putting on my bracelets, or helping or taunting each other, I felt how susceptible I'd become to that undercurrent.

A year or two before, my father and I had tumbled into an unexpected swirl of conflict about this almost-died/could-die-don't-let-it-happen. I was walking the dog at night and making calls. This was when Nana was still in her house, and Dad and I had set up a schedule so that one of us went there every night. My husband and children came once a week as we had done for years. My sister, with her two little babies two hours north, came as often as she could. Dad and Nana had already had their seven years without speaking. Their separation ended with a tearful reunion onto which Nana placed the condition that they never talk about what had passed. I told her then that I would have insisted on two years of couples therapy, and that if she wanted to reconsider, I could recommend someone. She thought the suggestion hilarious. We laughed, together and separately.

But, right, whatever. Dad came onto the duty roster, and

I thanked God. In fact, Dad and I didn't talk much either, except about what was in the fridge, or lightbulbs—and doctors' appointments. Always doctors' appointments: when, with whom, where. Who would take Nana, how to manage information-sharing among doctors and ourselves? How to keep on top of morbidity: it was an existentially stupid phrase, because mortality stays on top, no matter what. Each month Nana debated whether to let her hair grow out, asking me whether it was ridiculous for us to keep coloring it, especially when going downstairs got so hard.

"Nothing says we can't dye it upstairs," I said.

"Oh, thank God."

We spoke no more about it, just as we didn't talk about the losses that piled up and crowded every present moment.

Each doctor's appointment became a philosophical question, and with everyone involved, morphed into group therapy. If this specialist finds a problem that can only be solved by extreme medical rendition, perhaps too hard on the rest of her body, or likely to make other things break down, like a high-powered new carburetor in some '54 Ford in Havana whose radiator is strapped in with a piece of a coat hanger, what does one answer? If a person, such as Nana, who distrusts doctors, wants to ignore their advice, but comes up with her own prescription that requires the unqualified family member-caretaker to act against conscience or beyond competency, what does one do? If the family members disagree about problem-solving, and have no practiced habit of collaboration on life-threatening emergencies, how do they proceed?

Nana believed that her increasing deafness was a matter

of impacted earwax, for instance. (My dad, now in his eighties, says the same thing about his own hearing loss.) What
she wanted me to do was to warm "sweet oil," pour it into her
ear, and then, the next day, find some way to remove the wax,
probably with a bobby pin. These were our daily, weekly,
monthly garden-variety conflicts. But once when Nana was
still in her house, Dad rang me while I was walking our dog
at night to tell me that he was worried about the appearance
of one of her many moles. It looked like one he had spied on
his girlfriend; she'd gone to the doctor, found it to be malig-
nant, and had it removed. So he wanted me to be sure to get
her to see a specialist ASAP. We had two appointments lined
up, which was as many as I thought I could handle except in
an emergency. I'm not sure what I said, but it was definitely a
delaying phrase of some kind. I remember the warm evening,
and the sound of the rocks under my feet and how much I
wanted not to talk anymore, but just to walk silently.

My father shocked me by shouting into the phone: "This
thing could kill her!"

"Daddy," I said quietly, trying to pull back from wherever
we'd suddenly arrived, "Nana is ninety-nine years old."

(Eventually, Nana's doctor, the one her age, refused to
recommend a specialist, saying that although the mole
looked questionable, he thought that it wasn't growing fast
enough to threaten her life. If she'd been, say, fifty years
younger, then he'd say she should have it removed.)

But now, after the diarrhea episode, Nana had tricked the
devil again, as the saying goes, which is only funny when

one is speaking theoretically. Did Nana believe in the devil, a literal presence presiding over a literal hell? I couldn't tell. What I did not doubt was that each close call weakened her immune system, and left her more anxious to reestablish homeostasis, or some new balance on the high wire that life had become.

Still she'd outlived the hospice limits, and so now, we had no weekly nurse visits, no nurse on call, and no nighttime backup.

I was supposed to have given back the medicine box in the fridge, but I couldn't face elder care without a net. In case of calamity, I'd need to be able to administer a few drops of the morphine. And she was frail enough now that calamity lived with us, too.

Chapter 14

I told myself that this would be good for our daughter Zoë, who was still in middle school when Nana came. Our older daughter, Laura, had gone to Iowa with us when we helped my father-in-law at the end of his life. I told myself that death in the context of family, age, love, and care, rather than war and violence, was a fact of life that we should share with young people, or else how could they grow into their own stewardship of life?

But when we began auditioning day nurses to fill in around Gertrude, I realized that we'd brought more into Zoë's life than I'd had the sense to envision. The first few women from a nursing service started out their tours of duty well enough. They'd come in the morning, dropped off by relatives or driving old-model cars, each one having had difficulty finding the rectory next to the church on the leafy green Philadelphia one-block street our mailman called Shangri-La. I'd give them written or oral instructions according to how they said they liked to get information. When I came home from work, Zoë would give me an executive summary of the day. And because Zoë could get to me before

Nana, that was the gloss I took into the room with me when I went upstairs to hear from her how one woman or another had failed to do things right.

The eggs were cold.

The coffee was blech.

Can't hear 'em; they mumble.

They think because you're old, they can boss you.

Didn't listen.

Oh, she will never do.

I guess no one ever taught them how to do things . . .

Zoë began to characterize Nana's behavior with the nurses as "mean." She was mean one day or she wasn't mean. Nana still treated our children kindly, but when Zoë came home at three she found herself in close proximity to grown-up, professional women to whom she thought her great-grandmother was being unfair. What could she do?

Finally, the manager from the service called to talk to me. That's how I remember it. Like I was the parent of a kid in school who kept hitting people. But it's just as possible that I called her to stop sending young women once more unto the breach. In either case, I remember feeling ashamed on Nana's behalf. I'd seen this Nana at her office with "the tenants," and I'd experienced it myself after my parents separated. I'd heard this Nana with Pop-Pop, and mostly Photoshopped that side out of the frame. My sister called more often every time Nana felt ill, but if the young mother with two children under three was not able to drive two hours each way to visit, Nana spoke coldly to her too.

I complained to a few friends. They commiserated and tried to help. One recommended an Eastern European woman who she said had been brilliant with a hospice patient she knew.

Okay, okay, okay, I thought. Let's try a white woman. Who knows, maybe Nana will behave better long enough for this one to figure out what she needed.

Right from the gate, though, the Eastern European nurse let me know that she knew what she needed to do, thank you very much. I wondered whether also I whiffed surprise and some confusion at our whole mixed-racial deal here on the street with a tree right in the center and a pointedly capitalized definite article: *The* Oak Road. Yes, of course, she'd be happy to hear what I wanted to say, but first, she had questions.

"Does she need to be fed?

"Does she need to be washed?"

"Not exactly, but she needs help—"

"Can she operate the wheelchair herself?

"There's one down here on the first floor, I see; do you have another upstairs?

"Does she have a schedule?"

"Yes, she has a schedule, and here it is, roughly."

She read it too quickly. I hated when they read the schedule that fast, but then, I told myself hopefully, the other family had loved this woman, so stop with the snap judgments.

"And the schedule begins—ta-da!—with this Lumberjack Breakfast!"

She didn't appreciate my sense of humor. Hokay. Well, Nana didn't always either, so maybe that was a good sign, too.

"Now. I'll make it and we can talk to her—"

"I'll go up and introduce myself."

"No, let's wait, and you go up with me."

"I'll just go and survey the room."

"I wouldn't. She should not wake to a new person in the room." (Nana would say: "a stranger.")

"Well, if you insist . . . She eats all of that for breakfast?"

"Every day God sends."

When we went up, the new nurse surveyed the room. She'd seen better, her eyes signified, but she looked satisfied, talked loudly and began asking questions.

"Wouldn't you like to brush your teeth first, before breakfast?"

Nana rolled a Moby-Dick eye toward me, and I said again that it was much better to let her eat first, and then begin her morning ablutions. I said ablutions to make a little humor happen. No one smiled but me.

"Shall we go through the schedule?" I asked this as Nana ate.

"No, I shall read through it with Mrs. Jackson. Because I cahn zee dat she is bery barteegular."

"I have a hard time with accents," Nana said to no one in particular.

Each of them made a small signifying snort. I kissed the one, nodded to the other and went to work, because, well, as my friend Tina says, either it'll work or it won't.

At Art Sanctuary, we were planning for our ten-year anniversary. The centerpiece was to be a musical commission by Hannibal Lokumbe. The spectacular jazz trumpeter and

Grammy-nominated composer had come to Art Sanctuary's performance by the elegant jazz duo Dwike Mitchell—on piano—and Willie Ruff—on bass and French horn. Mitchell and Ruff had been to the Soviet Union in 1959, China in 1981, and the rest of the world in between. In the Church of the Advocate's French Gothic cathedral, full of Black Arts murals, Mitchell and Ruff played—and Hannibal whooped! Hannibal had been raised in Texas. When it got too hot for human beings to keep picking cotton, he said, they'd start singing. And then, somehow, they'd keep working. The music, he said, kept them alive.

Hannibal grew up in the church, with his mother's favorite songs, such as "I'll Fly Away." A prodigy on the trumpet, he began playing with bands at clubs when he was in high school, with the men coming for him in the car and promising his mother that they'd see to it he got his homework done on the road. So, he'd earned the right to whoop and holler when the music moved him. He loved hearing that we'd filled the church earlier in the day with high school students who had read excerpts of William Zinsser's book about the two men, which had come out after his *New Yorker* article about their private concert for the Beijing conservatory. Hannibal loved my stories about how the publisher Paul Dry and I had met with educators hawking the exquisite curriculum guide Paul had commissioned for our event. Zinsser had attended the high school matinee, as we called it, an eighty-something-year-old white man delighted to find himself surrounded by dozens of black and Latino kids, budding young musicians and writers, who asked thoughtful questions after the performance while dozens of others rushed to get photos with Mitchell and Ruff. One boy, a French horn player, had hardly been able to stay in his seat, he was so excited.

After the performances Hannibal told me that seeing and hearing these icons of black jazz playing at a black arts organization for mixed audiences of youth and older folks made him want to write something for us. For our tenth anniversary, we'd cobbled together funding for him to write one of his signature musical tributes to black heroes, this one to Father Paul Washington, the priest who had led the Church of the Advocate into the radical record by hosting Black Power conferences in the 1960s and the first-ever 1974 ordination of women as priests in the Episcopal Church. To get a sense of Father Paul, Hannibal wanted to talk to people who'd known him, so we set up meetings: with North Philadelphia neighbors and a former Black Panther member at the church; with the Washington family at their home; and, at a dinner in our rectory, with some Episcopal clergy who'd known, worked, and worshipped with Father Paul.

Nana's living with us overlapped these arrangements. I talked to her about them in the evenings, surprising us both with connections, such as our inviting Father Tom Logan, who had been Nana's priest, to the upcoming Hannibal dinner. She allowed as how she might stop down, probably not for dinner, but maybe just to be sociable before going to bed. Then she repeated something my mother-in-law had said years before. Nana claimed not to have understood it then, but did now. Edith's blunt honesty gave Nana permission to say the same thing: that her table manners weren't so good anymore to take out in public.

It was vintage Edith, my husband's biological aunt who, with her husband Carl, raised him from the age of three and adopted him. After Carl's death, we tried to get out there a few more times a year, as many as we could make workable. The year that Halloween fell on a weekend made a perfect opening. We could trick-or-treat in Iowa. Edith had never seen the girls' costumes, and our daughters had never gone house to house in their father's hometown of a thousand souls, scattered on either side of the original Lincoln Highway and Union Pacific tracks and surrounded by farmland. I invited Nana, because she'd said that one of the losses of aging was travel—anywhere.

Once a traveler's ambition was aligned with her capacity, it was a party. My mother-in-law had helped me learn this years before, when she and my father-in-law came to Philadelphia, both of them holding small bags—no heavier than they could carry comfortably—with Carl also carrying Edith's square toiletry case. When we suggested an activity, they weighed its possible enjoyment against physical effort, stress, and the sheer volume of newness. They said that they knew what was enough for them. And then they laughed, along with my husband, who translated for me later, that my ideas were too demanding. After that, we took a lot of drives, which let them see the city, and enjoy the baby Laura, who was easier to admire when she was immobilized in her car seat.

When we went to a McDonald's at the end of Edith's life, she and I tackled the ladies' room together for the first time.

Despite the ADA setup, though, she could not transfer from her chair. We found ourselves locked in each other's arms, struggling with her trousers. I felt her begin to giggle just before I heard her. At which point, knowing what would happen, Edith couldn't resist saying into my shoulder: "Just don't let me start laughing before I sit down!"

Like specialized dancers, we pivoted and hurled ourselves from where we were toward the toilet, which was one step farther and four inches lower than we expected. With my arms under her armpits, I hit the wall behind her and crouched. She plopped, and eye to eye, we screamed with laughter. Relieved, we untangled and continued laughing there in the stall until we cried. When Edith got enough control to breathe, she said, in that weighted Midwestern drawl that made one-syllable words swing like hammocks: *We just did make it!*"

Edith's silvery laughter was one of the attributes my husband described when he wrote about his adopted mother, who accepted the child the third time her sister-in-law came to her. As Edith told me, she wouldn't take him at first, because she knew she'd fall in love with that little boy, and his mother would return for him, and it'd break her heart. With Bob's father in the Pacific with the Seabees in the Second World War, the childless couple on their Iowa farm took the boy when his overwhelmed mother said she wouldn't come back. "That's when I figured he'd be better off with me."

As Bob's third wife, their third daughter-in-law, and the first black one, I figured the folks could have been excused if they'd had some early acceptance issues with me. But whatever their initial worries, they welcomed me with courtesy trained, I supposed, by the spirit of adoption that had created for them the family they'd hoped for.

Nana and Edith visited easily on the Halloween weekend we went to trick-or-treat in Iowa. I told Nana that in her early marriage on the farm, during the Depression, Edith had canned a hog, all in one day, and they were off.

"All in one day?" Nana couldn't believe it.

"Well, yes!" Edith said, laughing. "You had to."

They talked throughout the weekend about a world few people remembered.

After a couple of days with the Eastern European miracle worker, Zoë was waiting for me. "They had a fight," she said.

Zoë was already moving between worlds: her wealthy independent school on the other side of the back fence and Art Sanctuary's working-class urban arts after-school program. She was writing, playing music, and singing. These helped, while adding their own demands, as she handled a wide spectrum of social and emotional challenges, including race and class, social hierarchy and friendship. She had already announced, earlier in middle school, that she didn't actually believe in God, but she continued to acolyte, and substitute when anyone didn't show, and run to get keys when the opera company got locked out, or shovels when it snowed, or sweaters when kids were cold in Sunday school, or coffee when we ran out at a funeral. Because church was "the family business," and we lived next door to the store.

Ladysitting Nana became Zoë's second on-call job, especially in the after-school hours when we were not home yet. She came to see that anything could happen at any time, whether we were home with her or not. Death had moved in with us, along with Nana's increasing imperiousness. Zoë felt the weight of it.

It was not lost on me that I had been raised to please, and that the way to have peace in my house was to please Nana. Nor was it lost on me that I was insisting that our children do likewise. Some part of me, even farther down in the basement than the busy-bee-fixer-pleaser, was watching, and despising myself for it.

Then we met Karline. Related to Art Sanctuary's Haitian American marketing associate and to my Sunday school assistant, Karline swept in with disciplined jollity. When we talked about Nana's care, and I mentioned solutions to possible problems, she shook her head, pursed her lips, and answered in a drawn-out first syllable: "Egg-zactly!"

Karline studied Nana. She asked her curious, open-ended questions. She introduced, one by one, her own better ways of doing one thing or another. She made the bed, Nana said, so that you could bounce a dime on it. She talked into the microphone so that Nana could hear her, and she laughed, graciously, as Nana asked her to repeat things she said in her French Creole-accented English.

When I ask Karline now how it is that she succeeded with Nana after our string of competent, cheerful nurses who could not, she takes time to write back an answer that is both self-aware and specific:

> I tried my best to please her in every way. For example: she loved her breakfast to be served hot, alongside her coffee. She loved to talk and tell her story about her life, and I would always be contributing to the conversation. She loved to be entertained, especially with walks. Every Saturday afternoon, I was faithful to the practice of putting on Channel 12 to *The Lawrence Welk Show* [rebroadcast], which she loved to watch and hated to miss. In general, I was able to make her wishes my commands, without appearing obsequious. She loved my company and my personality. I especially remember how much she loved my accent.

Karline and Gertrude made two different yins; each in her own way made Nana's wishes happen, sometimes before she even knew that she wanted something. They were like the genie in the extravagant Chinese fairy-tale book with Italian Orientalist illustrations that Nana bought and read to me when I was young enough to absorb them into the archetype of my dreams.

"What if you could just think of something and have it appear?" Nana would muse. "What would you think of?"

We came up with favorite food luxuries, like blueberries out of season and peaches with heavy cream.

Later, when I reread the genie story, the young man seemed lonely. And now, more and more, so did Nana.

To some extent our family acted as Nana's yang, but we, too, expended a great deal of energy figuring out individually, and together, what Nana needed, what we thought would be good for her, what she wanted that felt unreasonable or was too at odds with our family culture to adopt.

In the early months, it was a power struggle. Some of what she thought were necessities were a definite No in our home: There'd be no boxes of cash tucked in a shoe box in her closet, for instance. A hundred dollars in her wallet in her purse in the night table: sure.

Other creature comforts were easier. Nana was very, very old: so in the winter she got cold easily. No, we would not turn up heat up in the entire three-story house to suit her. She said she'd pay. Didn't we want to be warm, too? Wouldn't that be better than running around in sweaters all the time? Surely we were cold.

"We can't stand it as warm as you need it, Nana, not for all day and night."

"I keep my heat to seventy. That's what I've done for years."

"No, Nana, your room stays at seventy-six. We had your room at seventy, but you got cold."

"Oh, get out of here!"

"It's seventy-six, Nana. I keep a thermometer in there."

"Oh, get out. My house stays at seventy."

"Okay."

"That thermostat is wrong. Let me see it."

Plus the fireplace!

When it was especially cold or gloomy, we started a fire in the morning for the nurses. Neither of them had ever tended a fireplace all day. Both gamely worked at learning, with Nana's kibitzing and their own observation and trial. Karline, I think, tended to keep the fire higher than Gertrude. I remember that her fire used five or six more logs a day than Gertrude, which I had to keep in mind each morning when loading them in.

At dinnertime, when Nana left her toasty bed-sitting room to come downstairs, we'd dress her in two layers. In the kitchen, we sat around the island while her wheelchair and tray were perched by the small cast-iron Swedish stove, her legs wrapped in a blanket, with one hot-water bottle under her feet and one on her lap. Sometimes she called the setup her high chair.

I disagreed when people said that living with an elder relative was like having a child, but in this way, it was: some part of my mind could not stop solving Nana's problems. The microphone and earphone setup, for instance, had taken me a month of shouting and missed cues to figure out. But every day I found myself watching us and thinking about how we were doing and what we were doing. It felt like writing a novel, where the actions of the lives of imaginary people whom I know, but not well enough, present themselves to me in every state of my consciousness. Sleeping, waking, meditating, concentrating on other problems, driving the car, meeting at work, teaching. Once committed, I couldn't stop it.

I noticed a never-ending rotation of Nana-care chores: the wheelchair dinner tray needed to be soaked. She'd given Laura and Zoë money and now was worried that she didn't have enough. Her old next-door neighbor had written her a letter, and she wanted me to sit down with her and write him a response.

There were household arrangements we'd made hastily when she came that we knew could be better. Also things to fix, like the newel post cap that needed tightening now that she clung to it as she climbed the three stairs from the landing to her upstairs wheelchair.

I could not clear my mind. I could not find a corner of the house that felt like my own. I couldn't write. The sleight of hand I'd employed for years to shuffle writing into my days and weeks no longer worked. After years of telling students and people at readings that you didn't need a fancy retreat, just a quiet corner and practice, I found myself unable to follow my own advice. Once discipline failed, I felt something just shy of desperate. More and more input with no expression.

Say it out your mouth.

I couldn't write.

Then, a funny thing happened. When I spent the night at a hotel after a lecture, I found myself scribbling away at the book I'd put aside since Nana's arrival. It just came back—the protagonist and his girlfriend and her son. It was, my husband said, "the geographical cure," and he suggested that I look for local hotel bargains to replicate the miracle.

This began my Friday night Hotwire odyssey. The first time I typed in $30, and the software sent me to a poorly lit room next door to lots and lots of headboard-banging. Lots. But I wasn't responsible for whether they were happy with what was happening, or for anyone's chlamydia or marital status. So I wrote. Like I'd written five years before when I'd started the project. The next week I sprang for $40. Hotwire then sent me to a room off the staircase in a downtown hotel, and I wrote some more.

At lunch I told my friend Helen about my success, and she invited me to spend Friday nights on her third floor where she and her husband Ted had for years hosted visiting students and artists. Once atop the steep stairs, the resident discovered luxurious privacy: a lovely room with a pitched roof, private bathroom, a deep closet and tiny anteroom. From late winter until the next fall, I went on Fridays after work, as early as 3 p.m. if I could sneak away, or as late as ten or eleven. Helen and Ted's hospitality to me was typical. When I came in, they'd often be hosting a few people for a dinner party—or a full-on party. Once someone called Ted's attention to the furtive front door opening. He shouted over the several conversations: "That's just Lorene going up to the third floor. Don't anybody say hello. She's not supposed to talk to anyone!"

In fact, Helen and Ted came once to the rectory to ladysit the grandmother I'd run away from and give the whole family another evening off.

Once I was able to get back into the book, I could write

at home during the week, just for an hour or two in the early morning, though being away, even just overnight, made me keenly aware that I was beginning to feel swirls of the paranormal in our house. A friend who works in non-Western healing came to the house to meet Nana and told me that the place brimmed with it. She told me that she could come with her son to burn sage to "clear" the house of its energy.

Bob frowned when I told him.

"Hey, no harm," I said. I didn't understand anything anymore, except that this friend wanted to come and help, and everyone helped in different ways, and besides Native Americans burned sage, and it might just be for us, or maybe for me like a ritual. I felt foolish trying to explain to my Episcopal priest husband why I was inviting a friend to clear the rectory of spirits.

"Just don't bring her in during Vestry meeting," he said.

Zoë had no objection to these decidedly extra-Christian practices and was excited to tell Laura when she came. They read tarot cards together, again with Bob's tight-jawed indulgence. Later, when things with Nana got particularly difficult, Zoë said that we needed to go buy some white sage bundles ourselves and do it again.

But that daughter, after all, had been swaddled in the paranormal since her birth—and before. Throughout my pregnancy with her I'd been writing about a fugitive slave, a fictional character based on a real woman who'd escaped in Philadelphia in 1855. Soon after several disturbing nights awake seeing my character as a baby, with a broken foot, I wrote a scene, based on research into nineteenth-century medical practices, where her father makes a rough, tiny splint so that she will be able to walk. Soon after, I experienced a seizure in the supermarket, more like some sort of mini-stroke than early labor, and was put on bed rest. It felt urgent that I finish the manuscript and send it out of the house to my editor, and put away the files, before she was born. I would not say, because it sounded superstitious, but I was afraid that the energy of the book, called *The Price of a Child*, would hurt her.

In fact, a couple of weeks later, she was born with a clubfoot. Doctors splinted it within five days. At six months, we agreed to surgery.

The novel I wrote during Nana's time with us, *If Sons, Then Heirs*, about the descendants of a black man who farmed a large spread in South Carolina into the early part of the twentieth century, had also changed in ways I didn't understand. Sage or no sage, Nana's spirits had haunted me, too.

Chapter 15

About that same time, the early reboot period, I still
drove to Jersey once every couple of weeks to check
on Nana's empty house: timers on lights, downed branches
after storms, sidewalks after snow. Sometimes the schedule
crowded up and I'd let two weeks slide by. As if she knew,
Nana would remind us of some detail that had to be attended
to. The old boiler would not be put off: the water level had
to be kept between two lines you could only see if you knew
what you were looking for. The glass was so old and discol-
ored that it looked as if mustard had been smeared on the
inside. The water level dropped according to how much
steam had been pumped through the pipes to the radiator,
and how much had condensed and drained back into the
boiler. Over fifty years, Nana had developed judgment that
worked like intuition.

Once, when she was still living in her house and a snow-
storm kept me from coming on my appointed day, Nana
had worked her way into the basement, sliding down step
by step on her bottom so she could get to that boiler. She
said it took the better part of the morning to figure out

each work-around: how to stand up once she reached the game room, then to turn the corner into the boiler room where it was hard to find a straight wall to lean on, then to ease down, close to the floor, to turn on the spigot, listen for the sound of rushing water, and turn it off when she thought it sounded like it was full enough. She couldn't see through the gauge window, of course, so sound was her cue. Or maybe not sound, since her hearing had deteriorated, but her ability to time the flow through the rhythm of repetition.

Nana had experience in conserving old things. Our lives were full of old things that she knew how to baby, as they said, so that they worked well past obsolescence. Nana's fridge, which she bought to celebrate the end of World War II, still perched in the small alcove in the kitchen and required defrosting more often now, but otherwise worked fine. Her washing machine was old enough to have a crank wringer attached over it, and the stove had a warming well where one could prove bread, soak oatmeal overnight, or make yogurt. Why waste money buying new?

The boiler was so old, she explained, that it could not take boiling dry. Nor could it take overfilling. I knew these things, of course, but not like Nana knew them. She maintained the boiler to avoid a freezing night, one that could really take out a ninety-eight-year-old living alone who was beginning to knock the phone extension off the hook without realizing it, and regularly struggled upstairs to sleep only to find that her calls wouldn't go through and figured that the circuits must have been busy. The boiler stood in for mortality. The woman who answered "How are you?" with "I'm here by being careful" knew that she was making mistakes, but knew that some mistakes she must never make, ever.

It was hot and dry in the boiler room, and loud when the furnace roused itself. There in winter, sheets dried in thirty minutes and towels in a couple of hours. In high school, when I read in Ralph Ellison's *Invisible Man* that a jukebox "lit up like a bad dream of the Fiery Furnace," I thought of the fire inside the tiny door of Nana's boiler. As a girl alive to miracles and afraid, after the Birmingham Church bombing, that America's hatred of black people extended to girls my age in church, I looked into that fire and imagined how in the Book of Daniel the three men with the black-sounding names were "bound" and thrown into a fire "seven times more than it was wont to be heated." And then when King Nebuchadnezzar looked in, he saw not three but *four* people standing up and walking around together, "and the form of the fourth [was] like the Son of God." Like ancient people who lived in a sacramental landscape, I squinted to picture a shadowy vision of the three Jews who refused to deny God in the face of kingly authority—and the Presence of God walking among them in the fire. They gave us the answer to violent American power; and they gave me the possibility of standing up, one day, to grown-ups.

So I had my own connection to the boiler, including a tiny trapped feeling when she sat at the top of the stairs in her wheelchair, and nodded with satisfaction and patted my hand when I came back upstairs from adjusting it each week or sometimes twice a week. Now that the house stood empty and we set the temperature to fifty-five degrees, I wasn't careful at all. I was frenetic. In midday I could cut the hour and fifteen minutes' round-trip to forty-five or fifty minutes. Then I'd water plants; change light timers (which likely fooled no one); check windows and doors, sump pump, boiler, and that sidewalks were clear of twigs and hedges. Miss Havisham takeout and delivery service.

One day, after a cold snap, when I knew that even at fifty-five the boiler would be working hard, I used a lunch hour to zip across the bridge. Just fill the boiler and go back to work. But something else had to be done when I got there. I don't remember what, only the sense of urgency ticked up a notch, and the funny, foggy feeling that I was not watching Nana's aged infrastructure with the care she had done. Flushing the toilets to make sure they still worked could fill me with dread. What would I do on one of these lunch break check-ins if the floor had flooded, or a door had been forced and someone was squatting in the bedroom, eating expired cans of cream of mushroom soup and watching *Mrs. Doubtfire*? What would I say to my father or my sister?

This particular day the boiler was lower than I'd ever seen it. I turned on the water and waited, but no water appeared in the glass window. So, I went upstairs to rush through the to-do list, which is what I usually did once the boiler had been topped up. When I got to the end of the list and realized I'd stayed longer than I planned, I left, quickly, to get back to work.

It wasn't until later that afternoon, after I returned to work in Philadelphia, that I realized that I hadn't turned off the water.

My memory has failed. I am fogged in, as if in a shame-filled dream, with disconnected images, each one troubling.

Image one: I'm back at Nana's house with Bob. The valves on two second floor radiators have blown out. Steam, first, then boiling water has overflowed and seeped into the floors. The corners of the living and the dining room ceilings have fallen in: white plaster in chunks on windowsills, the record-player cabinet, the dining room table whose legs had split, and which we'd bolted together.

We go down the stairs to the boiler. The smeary glass does not show the water level, as if, having disturbed the balance, I no longer deserved to know.

Bob finds the spigot and drains the excess water. We carry buckets of water from the boiler across what Nana called the game room and over to the sink next to the washer.

"Can you tell when the level is normal again?" he asked.

"No, I can't anymore."

I think I remember a guarded hope that the tough old boiler had pulled through.

Image two: I see myself alone, having hoped that the disasters had ended.

But, no, more of the ceiling has fallen in. I'm standing between the two rooms, the living and dining room, nostrils full of the smell of damp plaster, sobbing.

Image three: A different day. Although I don't remember calling him, the handyman, Roosevelt, is in the house with a helper, maybe his brother, mopping water into the sump pump. Water has overwhelmed the basement.

After working for Nana for twenty years, Roosevelt, too, had learned to anticipate her wishes. After working with her for twenty years, he could—and did. He called her "Mom." I think I remember him saying things like: "Mom wouldn't want to see this." I wondered whether he'd tell her, but, to my knowledge, he never did.

The oil company's plumber could not believe that he was getting to see such an antique furnace. He had it looked up and dated it to the 1930s. My cousin's boyfriend, a contractor who later repaired the ceilings, remarked on the quality and age of the plaster.

None of us told my grandmother. It felt dishonest and hypo-critical, and yet, I could not bring myself to do it. Of course, as one friend said, we should spare her the upset. But I also did not want her to start insisting on control, maybe trips back to the house for inspections, and endless questions. She already asked me about specific things: I brought her jewelry box to sit in her closet with her at the rectory. And I unhooked the spear-and-drop crystals that dangled from each of the pair of Czech luster lamps, wrapped them in newspaper, boxed them up, and put them into our base-ment, where no light shone through the cranberry glass or the prisms. Each week, something else had to be imported from the Land of Nan. We began a dance, as if to let pent-up anger drum into the rhythm. I told her that I could take care of her, but not her things. In fact, it would be a great mercy to us all if she'd let me sell the house.

Oh, no. Not her house. Nana would not consider selling. Why, that was her house!

I reminded her of the upkeep, the taxes, how old houses degrade if no one is there to use the plumbing and open and close the doors.

Well, maybe if it was too much for me, we could find someone else to do it.

I reminded her, gently, of how suspicious she was of anyone other than her tiny family going into and out of her house.

And she was sorry, so sorry to put this on me, and me with my foundation, as she referred to Art Sanctuary, and the family and the university and the church. What, she wondered, could she do to help?

Sell the house.

Oh, honey!

We sat together in the sun spot, each of us feeling put upon.

She tried again, using her signature hand-pat, right from my childhood. But what would she do, she asked, laughing, if Bob and I put her out?

Put her out? In all the years we'd been adults together? Where, where was the evidence? I did not mention, though it lay before me if not before us, a life together from baking to banking. And the last five years since her car accident: the not-a-stroke when we'd come daily for months, the dinners and drives, pickups and drop-offs, bill-paying, laundry.

Too bad, L'il Lorene.

And too bad, Big Lorene, originally named Rosalie Lorene. Was it after her mother died, I wondered, that Nana chose a new name and tucked her heart into herself? Now when Nana repeated her story about getting cotton for her mother to sew into a doll for her, I no longer heard recollection of a mother's protective love, but rather a set piece in place of memory, and embedded with loss. She'd lost her mother Lizzie, not the real woman, overburdened with births and miscarriages and child care, but a Victorian angel in the house, making a specific gift just for Nana; she'd lost the cotton fields; the South; the leisure of the landowning class; and like people with fewer material advantages, she'd lost childhood before she could grow out of it; she'd lost the illusion of, the protection of, wealth.

"When I go into the stores at Christmas and they play 'Toyland,' oh, my land, they could charge anything for those dolls, and I'd buy one!"

"I'm trying to remember the words."

She hummed the tune, eyes closed.

"You can never return."

"That's the one."

In the beginning, her mother had left her, and in the end, everyone would. It wasn't about us. The robust love Paul writes about in Corinthians, love that bears, believes, hopes, and endures, that love did not exist between us.

I made sure not to let her see or feel my hurt. So, now, each of us was walled in. It felt false, but easier.

"Bob and I will not put you out."

Nana considered.

Yes, she said, as if to convince herself, she felt loved here. Yes, she added, in the swallowed voice of someone arm-wrestled into submission, this was her home now.

But . . . and she hit on how to say it: What if something happened to Bob and me?

After that we added to our list of Nana jokes that she was happy to talk about death now—so long as it was not hers, but ours.

I reminded her that my sister had pledged backup; Carole would never see her turned out into the street, which was the Dickensian phrase Nana used. Carole could take her to Montclair, New Jersey, or work with her to find the best possible care scenarios.

Nana knew that, too. Sure she did. Strangled voice. Angry to be reminded of her dependence. When I asked whether she was secretly planning on getting well enough to go back to Collingswood, she sniffed and looked away.

How could she?

How could she not?

So, of course, she acknowledged. Everyone *was* taking good care of her . . . But she couldn't bear to sell her house. Even though she was at home with us, if we forced her to do it, she'd feel, well, she'd feel homeless. Couldn't we just see to it? It wouldn't be long . . .

That she'd been forced to acknowledge her own death was a white flag. Or maybe a final dodge.

We asked our older daughter whether she wouldn't mind house-sitting. Nana liked that she was providing Laura a rent-free home. From her point of view, she could provide something for one of her own, instead of the other way around. When Laura moved in, Nana remembered how I'd brought her to the house when she was just a few days old. We'd put her down to nap on the couch where we used to lay my sister to nap, with the same pillows positioned the same way to keep her from falling.

"And remember how we stood there looking at Laura?"

"Yep. And you said, 'Just think. A week ago this little person wasn't even here.'"

"Did I say that?"

"Yep."

From our point of view, Nana's care was now a full family obligation. At twenty-three, Laura was working at the University of Pennsylvania, from which she'd graduated, doing research for a film about African independence. She had life-long friends in Philadelphia, and at the end of the workday, if they'd get together for a beer, she could no longer join them. She later told me that almost none of her friends wanted to join her in a drive over the bridge past Camden to hang out in her grandmother's suburban house, two miles from the train back into town.

In addition, Laura came to the rectory once a week, from 5:30 until about 9 p.m. Nana looked forward to her visits, when they ate dinner together and chatted companionably, easily. Laura knew Nana. As when Carole visited, Nana could feel herself seen through eyes of love, and eyes of people who'd known her when she'd been, as she liked to say, "on her feet." Starting on Tuesday, Nana would start to ask whether it wasn't time for Laura to come babysit her.

"Ladysit, Nana," we said, "Laura's coming to ladysit with you, but not until Thursday."

Sometimes Laura was able to get Nana ready for bed, but inevitably, my increasingly anxious grandmother would call my name—her name—and ask me to stop in. If I didn't hear her, she'd call Zoë and ask her to get me.

Her bedtime ritual involved the tucking in of sheets and the precise aiming of a pedestal fan. We positioned the fan a few feet from the foot of her bed and aimed it, from that distance, at her face so that she could feel just a breath of it. Without the fan, she said, she felt almost as if she couldn't breathe. But getting the fan and the sheets and the blanket exactly right began to take longer and longer; the breeze was too strong; it wasn't quite on her face; now it wasn't strong enough. She apologized for the bother, but she couldn't get to sleep otherwise.

Because of the draft, she also required something around her neck. Nothing quite worked until I brought down from the closet a small, soft green-and-white fleece that we called the mommy blanket. When the girls were sick, I'd bring it out and tuck it around them at bedtime, after medicine and stories. In terms of healing, it was the closer. The mommy blanket had never failed to help the girls heal, because— and here's when they smiled no matter how sick they were— because they'd gotten better (eventually) every time! I told Nana what we called it, and how we all knew that there was no magic in it, but comfort. It was a tangible, purposeful talisman of care, like chicken soup with lemon. Nana adopted it.

"Oh, that feels good." She snuggled under it, catlike, once the fan was positioned. Then she'd ask me to repeat its name.

"I think you just like to hear me say 'mommy blanket.'"

"That's it!" She wondered as she was nestling, whether the girls minded her having it.

In fact, once it was clear that the small, worn fleece would not return to its place in the linen closet, Zoë asked, with mock indignation and just a shred of seriousness, how she would recuperate if she got sick?

"No," I said. "The girls want you to have it."

One night I remember rubbing her back after the tucking in. The woman who had once worn a size 18–20 after cruises and meals out was now thin enough that I felt each knob on her spine and every rib. Since her headphones were off for the night, I bent over and spoke directly into her ear. "See, I do them like this, and it helps, doesn't it? Don't you just want to fall off to sleep? It's the mommy blanket!"

"I never had a mother tuck me in," she said. "Not that I remember. All I remember is getting the cotton for that doll."

"You and I made dolls, too."

"Didn't we, though?"

The first doll I remember at Nana's was Little Lulu, named after a naughty comic-strip character that began in the 1930s and ran, in different forms, until 1969. Nana made it from a kit. Lulu had darts that gave her boxy cheeks and black yarn hair that Nana starched and rolled into curls that lasted for years. Nana taught me to make dolls by hand when my fingers had sufficient dexterity to hold the needle. We'd draw a paper figure, transfer it to cardboard, cut it out and draw its outlines onto fabric at night. Then you sew on the features: eyebrows, eyes, nose, and mouth. Lay her out staring up from the dining room table while you go to bed and dream about her and figure out who she is, who she's for, what she'll wear. You sew the seams the next morning, in good light, when you're fresh. Then there's the turning, pulling her right side out through the crotch, like she's giving birth to herself. Push out the hands and feet all the way using pencil erasers, admiring how the stitches hold. Then stuff her with cotton, like the cotton Nana's mother sent her to pick . . .

Nana's bedtime ritual lasted thirty minutes, unless some particular story had to be repeated. When the environment was juuuust right, as she used to say about Goldilocks and the porridge, she smiled and burrowed happily into the bed-clothes and mommy blanket. We were taking such good care of her, she liked to say, she couldn't die.

Chapter 16

Nana would not sell her house, but, despite my protest, she was intent to sell what was left of the Dickerson properties. In order to keep rents low, Nana had deferred maintenance from the 1960s when the city's Urban Traffic and Transportation Board threatened to redevelop Center City by running a Crosstown Expressway through "blighted" South Philadelphia. The route ran within blocks of the Dickerson properties. Civic groups coalesced to fight the proposal, arguing that the walkable city laid out by William Penn would become a suburban-era hybrid, that it would isolate Center City as its own wealth island away from neighboring communities. Including neighboring black communities. It would displace residents, mostly black. This was the area that W. E. B. Du Bois had studied for *The Philadelphia Negro* when the University of Pennsylvania had hired him but wouldn't let him teach undergraduates.

I never heard Nana talk about the Crosstown Highway's effect on Dickerson property values, and I'm pretty sure that she never joined in the civic protests. The expressway was abandoned in 1974. By that time many people who could move out already had. The Dickerson buildings chugged along, with Roosevelt now handling first minor, then larger repairs as cheaply as possible and fast. He also built relationships with residents. He knew them, so he could tell her who had gone to New York and installed an illegal sublet resident; whose stove needed repairing but feared saying it would mean a raise in rent; who had taken in a teenager whose music made the old lady downstairs go apoplectic.

I'd lived in a Dickerson apartment when I needed an inexpensive place to go, and quickly, when I separated from my first husband. Nana told Roosevelt to overhaul the third-floor apartment in a building on Christian Street, a few blocks from First African Baptist where in the early 1800s two black men sold themselves *into* slavery to buy out an enslaved man to serve as their pastor.

Although the building was rented as three apartments, Nana had never gone to the expense of converting it from the one-family house it had once been. So, when I came in, I nodded to the retired couple downstairs whose living room door was often open. On the second floor I walked through the hallway of the woman who lived there and usually closed the door of the room she was in, except the makeshift kitchen. Then I entered my own staircase, where I seem to remember the lone plywood privacy wall. Nana had Roosevelt build it especially for me. This was one of the nicest houses in the parcel, with welcoming neighbors who had worked hard to arrive at this place and valued it. My only complaint was the emergency rope ladder in a box on the third floor. In case of fire you were supposed to throw it out over the sill and climb down, Rapunzel-like.

"Look," I told a friend who came to visit. "If the place is burning down, who's going to have the presence of mind to climb down this thing?

"I should practice, but I'm scared." Then I took it out of the box. It crumbled in my hands, dry rot.

Nana had Roosevelt buy me a new one. He laughed as he installed it.

A year or so before Nana went onto hospice, the furnace caught fire in her office building, with its ghost-town storefront, Nana's Spencer Tracy office, and one remaining resident. No one was hurt, but the building became uninhabitable. Roosevelt was now Nana's right hand. At the rectory, as in her house, he came once a month with the rents, which they counted and recorded, and I banked. They missed each other, it seemed. Roosevelt would sometimes stay after the work to gossip with her or just sit and watch TV. I was glad for him, and glad that she had yet another connection of her own, the last work relationship. Gertrude and Karline would use the time to get dishes or laundry done.

Nana decided to sell to the man who had been buying from her, one building at a time for years. She liked working with him, because he made things easy. He knew the buildings and took them as they were, even the shells, without requiring her to make any repairs; he arranged the title searches, transfer of utilities—everything. One by one he had fixed up the properties so that the buildings around hers improved.

As the property values increased, so did his offers. When she sold a building, she could do urgent repairs on the others: roofs, boilers, chimneys. What was left to sell were fewer than a dozen buildings, most still occupied.

My sister and I talked about ways to keep the last Dickerson property together now that the neighborhood was being brought back to financial and architectural health. To the south, Philadelphia Sound composer and producer Kenny Gamble was anchoring whole-community resurrection with millions of his own dollars, bringing modest-cost housing, charter schools, and small-business development. To the north, east, and west, gentrification had taken off.

Some years before, when she made ready to sell, I'd asked her to let us manage them for her. They might be worth more than she was getting. Her response in the first instance was defensive. She'd managed these buildings by herself since before we were born. She'd cleared the mortgages. She'd never taken out loans. She knew what they were worth. But I had to remember where they were. Why, she remembered a time when you wouldn't be caught on Kater Street!

I told her what a renovated house sold for now.

But that's *only after it's been renovated!*

"Nana, we could renovate, too. And it wouldn't have to be total gentrification; we could renovate some and then upgrade the others."

"I don't have that kind of money! Do you have that kind of money?"

"We can find it. This one man is not the only one who can renovate a building."

"No loans. The properties may not be in the best shape, but they are free and clear!"

When I came at it arguing that keeping the property under black control was closer to the Dickersons' will, she became enraged. She had rented to black people who had nowhere else to go for fifty years, and it was a thankless job. She had provided more than a hundred and fifty scholarships. She didn't owe anybody anything.

This time, I tried another tack, an appeal to the personal. Wouldn't she consider holding back two buildings: one a tiny house where one lady had lived for forty-five years. She was in her eighties; why not let her stay?

Nana respected the resident, Mrs. Green, and had known her half her life. Mrs. Green's children were my age. Nana had seen them grow up. But more than that Nana knew that Mrs. Green had taken care of maintaining the building as if it were her own. It had cost the estate less than other properties and was in better shape.

The other proposal was both closer and more businesslike. Art Sanctuary had operated out of a North Philly church and needed its own headquarters. Why not lease the corner building where Nana's office had been? Two buildings deep, with a storefront and a small yard downstairs, and space upstairs for more offices, even an apartment for an artist residence or rental income, the Dickerson flagship building was perfect for municipal and state renovation grants. We did not have to look around for ways to improve the Negro race; arts and education benefited the race. For ten years I'd been building an organization *that benefited the race.*

"You know," she said, as if explaining a new thought to me, "your foundation *does* benefit the race."

The sale of the other nine buildings would proceed. Nana did not need a lawyer, she said, because she had done business with Mitch before, and he had always been "fair and square." Besides, she repeated, "he'll take care of everything."

They met; and he and I met. Having done so much business with her before, he was familiar with the deeds and the buildings themselves. He had a title and transfer company he favored, and a practiced set of strategies for raising the money. Nana asked me to write a letter that could be delivered to the tenants, giving them a couple of months' notice. Since that would likely not be enough time for many people, the new owner agreed to give them three months more.

Roosevelt came and visited, even though there would be no more rents. They talked a long time together. I cannot remember whether Gertrude or Karline told me that, but it seemed to make sense to me that they needed extra time. Roosevelt had worked on the Dickerson buildings from his early adulthood. She had trusted him. In this time of falling away, losing their tie would be hard.

In the 1990s, we'd compiled a complete list of the more than a hundred and fifty people to whom Nana had given Dicker-

son scholarships. I wrote to their colleges and alumni asso-
ciations and looked in the Philadelphia white pages to try
to find them for a celebration of Nana's tenure as trustee.
For months, the responses came back. Some lovely letters
saying that although the scholarships were not large, they'd
provided important gap funding, for books especially. Many
cards came back stamped deceased from the post office or
scrawled on the envelopes. The celebration ended up being
dinner out with Carole and me and just one woman, Sheila
Linton, a gracious retired middle school educator and new-
teacher coach. Nana said that she'd been glad to have seen
the list altogether, to have received the few reply cards and
well wishes, and to meet Sheila over supper as, let's say, a
representative of all the years' scholarship recipients. She
wasn't disappointed not to have more people, she said. In the
months that followed, however, Nana came to regret that she
hadn't kept in touch with the students.

Now, Nana rediscovered her nascent desire for the
estate's legacy. Under the new plan, 628 South 16th Street
would come back to life. She advised me to look up what may
have happened there. Her father had been so active politically, and she thought the Dickersons had been, too . . . After
years of assuming that she was hitched to a building that
would only go down, she began to imagine saving the corner-
stone. It captured her imagination. Every time I came into
the room she wanted to talk about it—Art Sanctuary and
628, her shorthand for the building's address.

—What was I reading?

—What was I writing?

—Where did I think I could get enough money to fix the furnace? She should have converted it to gas years ago.

—Two of the joists in the front were gone, at least two, and I'd have to get someone to bolt in sister joints.

—There's nice frosted glass in the stairwell; it might be worth something.

—I should be very careful about letting anyone into the storefront, because they might use it as a drug front.

However many times I told Nana we were going to gut the building, she could not envision it new, only repaired. So I nodded, and said that I'd take particular note of the joists.

We drafted the papers for the lease, Nana signed, and while her buyer worked to provide Nana with their practiced easy-transfer sale, Art Sanctuary's architect and our seasoned veteran grant writer and I began our work.

⁓

On the day of the sale, while Gertrude got Nana ready for our trip, I drove to South Philadelphia to meet Roosevelt in advance of the buyer's walk-through. I'd been dreading the day. Nana may have felt that she'd done all she could do for the residents. I did not. These buildings, with their humble brick faces fronting onto the streets, and their residents, Southerners who used agricultural metaphors and indirection in their speech by necessity—they had invited me to settle in South Philly when I first returned to the city as a young editor, back from a bruising affirmative-action stint, cynically run, at Time Inc. in New York, and stepping out of a wrong first marriage. I'd felt called to the place. Now our home, not the lovely stone rectory, but the brick row house where we'd raised our children, sat just four blocks away. This sale did not feel like what I'd been called to do. In fact, I felt as if I'd traded in my integrity for Nana's approval, for peace in the moment, if not harmony, in my home. There had been no good answers. Nana was legally the trustee; she would not give over control; she was feeble and forgetful, but in her right mind. I had kept from her the boiler explosion in her house in New Jersey, and I continued to pay our nurses twice what she believed. But she'd done these sales many times; there'd be no way, quietly, to stop them. And wrangling from her legal control of the estate while she lived across the second-floor landing: well, where was the God in that?

Still, as I parked in front of our own South Philly house and noted the old shutters, I heard my sister's voice from one of our earlier, agonized phone calls: "You were the one who told me how hard it is to build up and how easy to tear down."

Across from 628, Roosevelt was already waiting. He called me from his car.

"They're not gonna let 'im in," he said.

"Who?"

"Everybody. They got a lawyer. He told 'em the sale won't happen."

"They got the letters?"

Roosevelt assured me he'd gone to each apartment and handed each resident an individually addressed letter in September. Like he told me in September. Now it was November. He'd alerted them to the date of the walk-through. Younger people had moved or were moving. But not the long-term residents. He repeated the immediate dilemma. "The lawyer told 'em that since the sale can't happen, that they don't have to let anybody in for a walk-through."

"Aw, Rose," I said. "She's home getting dressed."

When I'd left the rectory, Nana had put on her game face. It had taken an hour for her to fall asleep the night before. Gertrude had committed to come to the realty office somewhere in the suburbs and stay with us until we got home. "The sale is going to happen."

"Some of these people, I've known them for twenty years, and they won't let me in."

We sat silently for a while before he said, "Maybe they'll talk to you."

We went to the doors of three or four people I knew. Same story. I asked them to give me the name of the lawyer. One talkative old man named Walker said through a closed door that they didn't have to tell me the lawyer's name. I walked across the street with Roosevelt as the tiny village watched us from their windows.

Just around the corner an elderly lady sat by the window, winter and summer. We hallo'd through the screen every summer—*"How you doing?" / "Here by the grace of God"*—and when I walked by in the winter, even if I couldn't see her, I'd lift my hand in a simple salute. She lifted the window a crack, told me the same story, but agreed to tell me the lawyer's name after consulting with a younger relative in the next room.

The lawyer was listed and answered my call. I assumed people were still watching from nearby. He told me that residents got in touch when the heat was not turned on in October. On October 15, according to law, she had always turned the heat on, and on April 15, she had always turned it off. October was cold, and they'd had no heat. Naturally, after receiving the letters, and the office having been damaged and closed, they assumed something terrible had happened. And they were cold. And angry. The lawyer had called the office phone, but it had been turned off. Then he found her house in New Jersey and called that phone, which was also disconnected.

But Roosevelt had brought the mail from 628, and I picked up mail at her house, I said. Why hadn't he written?

He ignored the question. Instead he answered that he was pretty good at finding people, and having gotten no response, he had assumed that she was dead.

"She's not dead. She's living with me and getting ready to go to the sale in a few hours."

"Is she sound of mind?"

"Sure."

"Well, then the sale is legal."

"You told the people they wouldn't have to move."

"Yeah. That's what I thought."

When our buyer came up to us on the sidewalk, I explained the situation. Mitch was as much salesman as builder, and from years of working on Dickerson buildings, he knew the residents better than I did. He'd try himself. He went back to Walker's building. I stood nearby, ashamed, as Roosevelt opened the front door and residents stood to block their way in. Mitch told them quickly the lawyer's error. I think that's what I heard. Then scuffling and raised voices. Walker smoked cigars, and the raggedy, bluesy edge of his voice made a rough descant over Mitch's staccato insistence. Then I heard Mitch saying, "Do you know her voice? Would you know her voice if you heard it?"

"Course I would, but the lawyer said she had to be gone . . ."

In the gloomy November hallway, Mitch pushed the speaker button on his phone and held it aloft. Nana's voice spilled out over their heads. I could hear she'd grabbed the phone herself, without waiting for Gertrude, who was probably emptying her wash water and laying out her clothes. Without earphones and mic, she couldn't hear, so she nearly brayed. "Hello? Hello? Who is this? Who is this calling me?"

The people in the hallway hushed.

Mitch came out to us, saying that he knew the buildings, anyway, that there were always nasty surprises, but probably not more than he anticipated. He'd see me later at the transfer office.

Roosevelt drove me to my car, recounting the morning's drama. I drove to the rectory and loaded Nana and her chair into the minivan. Gertrude climbed into the rear seat and made pleasant conversation while we drove. Nana had the glasses we'd gotten at the low-vision clinic. I withdrew into myself to stifle anger and loss smeared with shame.

At the office, a young white woman handed papers to Nana, who looked to me. I pointed at the line where she was to sign. Mitch told me that he'd really wanted the corner building for his office and was sad not to have it in the transfer. I told him that it would be a good neighborhood anchor for his other buildings.

When we got home, I could hardly talk.

"You told Roosevelt not to turn on the heat," I said once we were upstairs and ensconced in her seventy-six-degree room.

"Well, I figured since we were selling, and we let them go without paying rent in lieu of giving them back their deposits, that it would save money."

"It was cold."

"Oh, stop it. It wasn't that cold."

"You've had heat. I've had heat."

"You should be happy it's over. Instead you're making me miserable."

We deposited the check in the Dickerson account, after holding out 10 percent for Nana, and enough to renovate the house across the street from the headquarters. The remainder created the Dickerson Fund, using the wording of the original will, at The Philadelphia Foundation, a community philanthropy. The Dickerson office building and storefront would be renovated to house Art Sanctuary; the fund would support the building and programs there.

A few years later, after Art Sanctuary's grand opening, after the storefront gallery had displayed a variety of shows, and hosted everything from chamber music to capoeira, and established an after-school program, I saw Walker and a friend sitting, where they had for years, in the afternoon sunshine across the street. They'd brought lightweight folding chairs, and Walker, at least, had his butt of a cigar. Thinking that he'd be within his rights to curse me, I crossed the street to say hello.

He said that he had a new place to live. It was all right. He was doing, and thanks very much for asking. But this had been his corner for so long, he liked to come back for the afternoon sun.

A hulking older man hunched over a raggedy bicycle rode by and saluted the shiny new gallery window, which had been boarded up most of my life: "Took fifty years, but it was worth it!"

Walker chewed his cigar. The sun shone on him and his silent companion and me, plenty of sunshine for all of us. I remember regretting that the municipal grant I'd hoped would cover a solar panel on the Dickerson building roof had been revoked, for no good reason. But the sun still shone and warmed all our bones.

Then, just when I was about to leave, Walker said that he'd seen the notice in the paper when Nana died. He'd cut it out, he said, and he kept it in his Bible.

Chapter 17

If Nana's time with us were a symphony, the greater part of it would be the second movement, *andante*, after the sale, and after she lived too long to stay in hospice. Our lives sped up to accommodate the daily urgency of her care, but she herself settled in, and for a few seasons, the pace of change slowed to one she could, we all could, absorb. Gertrude came one day, then Karline the next. I paid them, more than Nana knew or would have approved, thus continuing the family tradition of financial secrecy. By opting for control over candor, I felt as if I were continuing to trade in my integrity. Every now and then Nana chuckled about how dear it was of Gertrude to give her "the family rate," and we said nothing.

My father, who had once been an acolyte, began to attend church regularly for the first time I can remember. He told me later that this was his way of supporting Bob. After church, he'd stop to see Nana. We set a small table on the west side of the room with sandwiches, and he'd stay to have lunch with her, tête-à-tête, and maybe watch TV. Hearing their voices together regularized Sundays. For years, we had gone to her house on Sunday afternoons. Now, even though she lived with us, she could still have her own special Sunday-lunch family visit. Even the residual tension between them gave off its own familiar reassurance.

They were doing so well that I asked them if we could leave them alone together. Each hesitated a moment before agreeing. Just for a couple of hours, I said. This might add another regular ladysitting appointment, especially welcome on Sunday, which had no wiggle room, ever. I can't remember what I did or who with that afternoon. I did think that if we could schedule Dad, this couple of hours could be a time for me to be alone with Zoë, even if it were nothing more than watching a show.

I returned hopefully. Dad smiled and said he needed to leave. I walked him to the door. "Everything okay?"

"Sure."

But when I went back upstairs Nana grabbed my hand. "Please," she said, "don't leave me alone with him again."

"But why, Nana? What happened?"

It was nothing she could point to, she said, and "I know how this might sound since he's my own flesh and blood, but I don't feel safe."

There was no talking her out of it. Nana wanted me to agree that her feeling was justified, but all I could do was reflect on the fact that they'd never properly fixed whatever had gotten them off track for seven years. And it had been Nana—I'd seen her do it—who had forbidden any discussion of hurt or harm or healing. So they'd hobbled on, having amputated that chunk of their lives, and ignored the phantom pains that coursed through empty air between them.

That night I told Bob. He went in to sit with Nana and told

me to take an hour with Zoë in the third-floor room where she went more often now.

Bob began his fourth year as rector, the church and its activities were growing: a Saturday evening dinner and mass in the rectory, Wednesday prayer and discussion groups. Another group worked on how the church could become a better institutional neighbor. We began a speaker and performance series. A printer in the congregation created beautiful brochures that we sent throughout the neighborhood.

Zoë's performances were gearing up, at school, in afterschool, in piano practice and recital schedules. Although she handled schoolwork with poise, more and longer practices and requirements demanded growth, technique, memorization, and surfing her several communities.

Now that Nana had become Art Sanctuary's landlady, she wanted to meet Hannibal and hear about his project. When he came to the rectory for our clergy remembrance dinner, he brought with him a Southern courtesy my grandmother loved. She asked him questions about his music and his travel and pronounced herself very impressed by his accomplishments.

Nana added Hannibal to the story of our collaboration, calling him "your friend, the musician." Nana had never followed the civil rights movement into Black Power and had certainly never driven to North Philadelphia for any of the conventions in the late sixties and early seventies. But now, when Hannibal talked to her about these historical events, in the context of Father Washington's life and at a distance of thirty years, well, she was all for it! Her father, after all, had been a race man.

Parishioners included Nana in invitations, too. They made over her at coffee hour, which she attended in good weather or when we held it in the rectory. We got coffee hour ready the day before, and she and Karline would come down to help with preparations. Nana would urge me to "hold some back for the family," especially her favorite sweets. I'd argue that I could not set out a pie or cake missing the first quarter. She suggested putting individual slices on saucers. I countered that the only way I could work Sunday school and coffee hour in the house was to go self-serve buffet. And then Karline would suggest slicing the cake and laying the slices in a row on the platter, and we'd laugh.

"You are clergy family now, Nana. That means give it away!"

"Well, not all of it. That's not what God wants."

"That's exactly what God wants!"

Parishioners asked after Nana when she wasn't there and told her that they were praying for her when she did come. During the week, we sat in on Roland's practices occasionally, and once even visited the Bel Canto Opera practice.

"Their voices are just beautiful," Nana said as we rolled out to the wheelchair ramp. "But aren't they *loud*? I could hear every word." She reached up and patted her ears to check before she said, "And I'm not even wearing my earphones!"

Karline made it a mission to take her out regularly. Nana, who had gardened enthusiastically around her suburban house, especially loved The Oak Road's spring bloom: pink, white, yellow, trees, bulbs, shrubs, one after the other, each on nature's rolling schedule, with examples of each on vivid display.

But The Oak Road's lush flora brought out fauna. For two days we stalked a bat from one slick hiding place to another, hoping to keep it from hiding in Nana's room during the day and then bouncing off the walls at night. I opened the first-floor fireplace flue to encourage a sooty squirrel to come downstairs rather than scratch at the damper in Nana's room. It made stops on the dining room shade, which it shredded on one side, and behind the microwave, before Bob and I herded it outdoors. Brooms were involved, and a close-weave laundry basket and maybe a small carpet.

Nana said almost every night that mosquitoes had always been attracted to her, and because it was true, we scoured the room in the evenings, which lengthened the bedtime ritual. I found myself staying up later to have a few minutes' check-in with Zoë, who stayed up later than we did, or Bob.

But one night an especially diabolical bee evaded the evening roll call. It found its way into Nana's room, and sometime at night, landed on her face. Maybe it was aimed at the sweets under the plastic wrap on her night table. Maybe it was dying and dropped from one of the blinds. Over the next weeks theories proliferated. But however the MFer got in, it made the error of stopping on Nana's face, where she smashed and killed it, despite being 101 years old and sleeping, or maybe sleeping, at the time. Before dying, the bee stung at both her hand and cheek, but couldn't manage to sink the stinger into either surface. Nana began to shout my name. Zoë, who slept directly above, was the first to hear her, and flew down the stairs.

"Get your mother," Nana shouted. "Lorene! Lorene! Lorene!"

It's an important moment in our ladysitting family life. Each time we recall it—*Oh, my God, the Bee!*—Zoë tries to place it exactly: eighth-grade spring, ninth-grade fall? Did she have soccer the next day, or was it some other sport where she sat out on the field and told her friends? I never can place it—first summer or second? The Bee is shorthand. It stands for the nights when something frightened Nana or bit or buzzed or swished or fell and clunked and reminded her of her extreme vulnerability and homelessness; for the time when she got up, bypassed the potty chair, felt her way to the wheelchair, maneuvered thirty feet to the end of the room, and fell into the closet looking for the bathroom; for the nights when it was too cold or too hot; or for when she asked to try overnight adult diapers hoping to sleep through, but then could neither stay asleep nor remove "the contraption" when she went for the potty chair as usual. Then, there were the nights she woke up wet.

In any event, on the Night of the Bee, Zoë ran to get us. Up, up, up. Shouting behind her. *Alarum* without and within.

"What? What happened?"

"She said something bit her."

"Where, Nana?"

"Oh, my God. Don't ask me questions."

Sleepy mind whirred awake: Bat? Squirrel? We'd never

had rats in this house. Raccoons lived in the woods near us. Opossum don't generally bite. Rabies? But the dog lay next to us unperturbed. Or at least he had been.

Oh, a bug. Lights on. We're here. We're here. All of us round the hospital bed, inspecting everything. I inspected her face and hand. Bob and Zoe inspected the sheets and windowsills and floor. Yeah, turn on her high-intensity light. Close the door. Sorry, Bee, you didn't bumble into a Buddhist house. Christians live life with a dead Jew on a cross. We are a bloodthirsty lot. Find the bug and kill it. Because without a carcass there'd be no way to know whether it would wait for us to leave and then dive-bomb her again.

I do remember thinking on these nights of the story Nana liked to read and tell us when we were children. An old woman found a crooked sixpence while sweeping, took it to the market to buy a little piggy, and walked the pig toward home until they came to a stile, which the little piggy wouldn't jump. The old woman implored Piggy, as I wanted to implore Nana, to jump over the stile so that she could get to bed.

But bees can only sting once, and then they die. What if it wasn't a bee, but a wasp?

There was ice and baking soda, like she put on us when we were little, and salve and coo-ing.

And then, just when some of the puffing had gone down and Bob had found the dead critter, and showed it to her—dead, dead, dead—and we thought she might be calming down, Nana turned her head to the ceiling, opened her mouth, and launched into a full-on wail: "As if I didn't have enough problems already!"

Zoë's eyes flashed behind her glasses. She almost laughed

outright, but looked away, just after letting me see that she'd branded the statement for life. Now and then, when one of us is feeling sorry for herself or encountering a bump in the middle of some serious challenge, we will wail it—*"As if I didn't have enough problems already!"*—and then remind ourselves of being tired, riled up. Each of us was temporarily out of resources, she of the ability to cope, we of compassion.

Then, in spite of, or maybe because, I'd snorted a little, and felt guilty, because it was getting funnier, I sent Zoë back to bed, heard her chuckle on the stairs—and then, *Shazam! Hot damn!* remembered the purloined hospice emergency box that I had kept at the back of the fridge. Generally, she was suspicious of any medicine beyond her two high blood pressure pills and, thanks to Nurse Barbara and blessings upon her, one stool softener. But I remembered morphine from when Zoë had been hospitalized at six months for surgery on her foot. That first night they had given it. Just as it started to wear off, I'd see her eyes start banging back and forth as if she were looking for escape. I carried her to the nursing station; they dosed her, as they said, and her eyes, still fastened on me, told me that she had returned from panic, back into my arms.

I asked whether Nana would take a few drops of medicine to help the pain. I was pretty sure this would help, just a few drops, not a pill. How about that?

Anything.

The tiny bottle is clear glass and the morphine a deep aquamarine. The dropper was a technology Nana recognized and trusted; the liquid, which I remember putting under her tongue, tasted bad. This was medicine that came correct, like she remembered from childhood. It worked within a minute or two. The pain subsided and her breathing relaxed.

The next morning, we found the stinger folded into her sheets.

To try to interrupt Nana's anxiety about the possibility of another bee-apocalypse or wasp or spider attack, we turned the story into one of triumph: Once again, she had lived to tell the tale. Creatures in neighboring hives had heard the news. They flew past the French doors of the rectory's second-floor parlor with little wings all atremble, returned to the hive and did their little information dance: Nana One; Bee Zero.

The other tale, about the old woman and the pig, was one I reminded her of after that. We lobbed it back and forth in a gentle game of memory and exegesis, as we did when I was a girl, when Nana had infinite patience for the long English story of rural life and possession and hardship:

"But the piggy wouldn't jump the stile, so the old woman went a little further until she met a dog. And she said: 'Dog, dog, bite Pig, because Piggy won't jump over stile, and I shan't get home tonight.'

"I bet she was tired, don't you think? And she'd been to the market. And there weren't any cars or buses . . ."

"And it was nighttime."

"And it was nighttime, and dark, and maybe getting cold . . ."

"And she was hungry."

"Very hungry! She didn't have a supermarket, did she? Or a refrigerator?"

183

"Or stuff you could take with you."

"Maybe a lunch. Maybe she'd baked some hard bread and wrapped it in a kerchief . . ."

"Ew. But she already ate it."

"Right, and the rest of her supper was home! But Dog wouldn't bite Pig, so the old woman went a little further, and she found a stick, and she said, 'Stick, stick, beat Dog. Dog won't bite Pig, Pig won't jump stile, and I'll never get home tonight.'"

Sometime around third grade and long division, and after President Kennedy's assassination in Dallas, I had lost patience with the long row of refuseniks in the story. Now, it was time for patience again.

The old woman kept going "a little further": she found a stick, but it wouldn't beat the dog; Fire, but it wouldn't burn the stick; water, but it wouldn't quench the fire; an ox, but it wouldn't drink the water; a butcher, but he wouldn't kill Ox; a rope, but it wouldn't hang Butcher; Rat, but he wouldn't gnaw the rope; and a cat, but he wouldn't kill Rat. We added one of the characters, and then one of us would forget another. And how did that old woman manage to get them all going? Did she get a dog to go after the cat?

No, the dog is already at the front, *not biting Pig* . . .

But the shortness of breath that we'd noticed that night came on more quickly now. And she more easily slipped into gloom. Karline and Gertrude kept track of subjects that cheered her most reliably and deployed them, along with walks in the sun, yogurt, cookies in the afternoon, fresh linen, and gossip about alumni party preparations for the start of the school year at the headmaster's house next door. Once Nana mentioned interest in the newcomer black presidential candidate from Chicago, however, we'd struck on a piece of news, like that of her grandchildren, that pulled her like a magnet back to the present day.

"How's our young man doing?"

Karline, especially, kept her up to date. I'd hear Nana asking her, about the progress of Barack Obama's campaign during the Democratic primaries.

"Oh! You know what?" Karline answered with enthusiasm. "I think he won *another* state!"

"*Whaaaat?*"

"Let's check and see which one!"

On June 8, 2008, after Hillary Clinton formally ended her campaign and endorsed Obama, Karline began a running joke that Nana loved to hear repeated.

"I love this country," Karline play-shouted. The *r*'s spun as if riding on a greased ball-bearing, and her soft *a*'s were wide-open and flat, making Barack Obama's name sound as African as it began.

"He wins, and what does Hillary do? Does she tell her followers to run over to his offices and beat everybody up? No! No! She says, 'Good fight. I don't like to lose, of course, but the people have spoken. You win.' Just like that: You won.

"I love it!"

Chapter 18

Imagine a wheelchair on a high wire, poised on one wheel, perfectly balanced to defy gravity, and waiting below: the triangle of old age, sickness, and death that drove Siddhartha from his throne into the wilderness.

The exhilaration and wonder come from knowing that if the balance involves human flesh and human effort, it will tilt, wobble, change, and fall.

Another story we told between us: I was a little girl, not feeling well, and so sleeping next to Nana in Pop-Pop's bed, the two rolled together each day, but made up separately, each twin top sheet tucked into the center crack. Nana and I were each sleeping, and she was dreaming about ice skaters—Nana herself didn't skate—gliding around the ice to *The Skater's Waltz*, which she loved, and I didn't, and everything was so peaceful and graceful, and then all of a sudden *Balumph!* She woke up thinking the skaters had crashed and found that I had fallen out of bed! Here she was awake and worried, and I was lying "sound asleep on the floor!"

Now, she was falling, over and over, one step after another, and sometimes she knew it, and sometimes not. The shortness of breath had come on slowly, but we all noticed it before Nana did: Gertrude, Karline, Carole, Zoë, Bob. As you watched her you could feel it: the shallow exhales leaving too-small pockets for new air to force into; the exertion of simple movements, the force required to inhale. Nana was pulling in life through a cocktail straw, with lots of co-morbid chasers. Her mind seemed less sharp and eager. She was becoming more suspicious and afraid.

We asked Holy Redeemer to send someone to come and assess her condition. They said that the degenerative disease of her heart was on the move again, busily degenerating. Nana was placed back onto hospice. Nurse Barbara resumed her weekly visits; we were granted 24-7 access to Nurses on Call. The five-day Family Respite program and other in-care facility options were back in play, although we did not plan to use them. Nurse Barbara ordered us a second emergency care box, since I did not tell her that I'd never returned the first. Also oxygen. No jubilant, jocular references to beating the odds. Instead, we spoke of comfort. The oxygen was to help Nana feel more comfortable. We parroted the phrase, hoping to convince Nana to yield to wearing the nasal cannula.

But from where Nana sat, the oxygen was one more damned thing to weigh her down. Almost the last straw, as she said. Glasses from the low-vision clinic; earphones with their wire to the mic; and now oxygen tubes.

"There's no more room to hang anything on my face!"

"Nana, looks like you need another pair of ears."

"How am I supposed to use the potty with all these?"

"Here, Nana, let me move the tubes."

"I can't tell which wire is which."

And so we rowed on, all of us in our little boat, as if out to sea, with Nana strapped in at the helm, me with a mind that kept churning out metaphors, as if it would help me understand better the swirling changes, or help me to feel less trapped.

Zoë began ninth grade. I leaned on her more heavily. One Sunday afternoon I left her to ladysit while I went out for the afternoon, and when I returned Nana complained that she was hungry. Hadn't Zoë offered her something to eat, as we discussed?

Zoë told me Nana had asked for cheese and crackers. Zoë made a little snack plate, with cheese and crackers on one half, and grapes and a brownie on the other, for *lagniappe*. She'd seen me do it; she'd done it herself before. Nana had been dismissive and rude, finally, in a fit of pique, saying that she'd take a couple of peanut butter crackers to tide her over instead.

I knew it had happened as Zoë said. I knew that she had done her best, and that Nana was becoming unreasonable, even with her younger great-granddaughter. It's a parenting moment I regret, like punching through Laura's wall nine years earlier. I told Zoë that her job when I was away was to figure out how to take care of Nana so that Nana felt cared for, full stop, not to some standard that *should* have satisfied a reasonable person. I had for years urged the girls to "use your resourcefulness and initiative." But there had been humor involved. They quote the phrase back to me at odd moments and we all fall out laughing. That autumn the humor dropped away. I remember saying the phrases I used at home and at work with everyone who had to answer to me: *Figure it out. Make it happen.*

Zoë reminds me now that I also told Nana that Zoë should not be treated dismissively, because, like the rest of us, she was working hard to do her part. I remember Nana backing down from cold indignation at having been mistreated to a more pitiful stance of having been misunderstood. Of course, she knew Zoë was doing her best, and, of course, I should be able to run out on the weekend, or go to work without having to worry about the old lady. Maybe she hadn't heard Zoë correctly. But now she was so awfully hungry . . .

Nurse Barbara explained that less oxygen to the organs and, more importantly, to the brain would continue to affect Nana's cognition and mood. I replaced the oxygen cannula and explained to Nana that her brain needed oxygen like her belly needed food.

So, we haggled: if she put on the damned nose thing, I'd bring her a liverwurst sandwich, but just half so as not to ruin her appetite for dinner.

Hannibal told me that the tenth-anniversary piece had filled his head with wonderful music, which he would call sometimes and sing to me, in one big, blurry burst of music energy, with his flip cell phone perched on the piano. Our conductor, Donald Dumpson, had been a principal interpreter of Hannibal's other new choral music. He reassured me, as the deadline passed for us to receive the score, that Hannibal would turn in the music late, but that it would be wonderful music, and that Donald would do everything in his power to bring together our three choirs and the soloists and quintet. Hannibal himself would play trumpet solos.

Then a fine musician and educator from the Creative and Performing Arts High School rang to say that she'd have to pull out her choir. The other music teacher at the school had taken ill and was not allowed back to teach for the fall. That meant that this one choir director was teaching, coaching, leading, everywhere, each period. She'd added the Art Sanctuary commitment for the sake of introducing the young musicians to Hannibal and to performing a new work, but now, she'd be unable to handle the extra practices and travel. None of the other elite school choirs would agree to jump onto our moving train at this late date—September commitment for a November performance. Only the choir director and pianist at West Philadelphia High School would join us. "No one ever asks us to perform outside of our walls," she said. "We need this."

Hannibal finished the score and came to Philadelphia to live in the bare UPenn dorm room we secured. Every morning at seven or so, like athletes, the West Philadelphia singers arrived to sing together, even though as the day matured, their high school filled up with conflict, punishments, and even small, angry acts of arson. In turn, Hannibal walked to the high school several mornings a week. He listened to the choir, sang and played with them, and promised them that they would perform the piece. With love and passion, he told them: "You *are* music!"

We created a special matinee performance for other high school students at the modern High School of the Future, with its well-outfitted auditorium. The kids would sing, their teacher would play, and Hannibal would accompany them on two pieces of the new work, all introduced by the generous Tamala Edwards, who, like Rick Williams, Ukee Washington, and several other black TV anchors, lent our young people's performances the confirmation of their emcee ease and celebrity.

I sat in on one of the choir's early morning sessions and felt the restorative energy of young people and a committed adult singing together every morning, it seemed to me, to save their lives. Over and over they practiced their two pieces for the performance, even incorporating a few last-minute changes to "Rejoice" the adult choir would not.

I give thanks for my life
and for all it means to me

All the pain and the joy
it's a sacred mystery

Too profound to waste
in the grave of hate and fear

For the number is set
each smile each step each tear

So rejoice in the gift
of living one more day

Give to life all your love
before you pass away

Rejoice, Rejoice
Rejoice, Rejoice
Rejoice, Rejoice
Rejoice, Rejoice

Even now, just rewriting the lyrics, I can hear the tune, and the kids' voices with their teacher's percussive piano accompaniment, and Hannibal shouting encouragement into the mix.

Our church organist played it, too, for the choir to sing. Good Shepherd had bought a new piano, and Roland was playing everything on it, including a concert featuring Rachmaninoff. Nana attended the concert given to bless the new grand piano. Just before it, I rolled her into one of Roland's evening solo rehearsals where she could sit right next to the piano in the partially dark church and feel the vibrations as well as hear the torrent of notes. She proclaimed it as good as one of her record albums.

At the actual event, full of parishioners and visitors, she was fêted nicely. At the reception they offered her food and drinks and compliments. Like some elder royal, she accepted their tribute: she performed a serene smile, chuckled a little, and adjusted herself in her chair. Occasionally, someone would pull up a chair, pick up her microphone, and hold a proper conversation with her. We watched her from a distance and enjoyed the moment of psychological rest, fewer now, and more precious.

During this time, Obama's amazing presidential campaign continued apace. In October John McCain took the microphone from a supporter and said, kindly and quietly to her, that Obama was not an Arab. We talked about all of it, and whether it was possible? Now and then Nana said that she wished her father could be here to see it. I had registered her to vote in Pennsylvania. How had that happened, she wanted to know. I reminded her that we had registered her for the primary, but that the paperwork, along with that of thousands of Pennsylvanians, had been held up in the mail, despite our making the cutoff. Every few days, as she got more excited about the campaign, she repeated that she wished she could vote for him when the time came, and I told her that she could.

—How would we manage it?

—How had we switched her from Republican to Democrat?

—From New Jersey to Pennsylvania?

—Where would she vote?

—Oh, right here at the church? They brought the voting machines right into the parish hall? Right up the driveway, under her window?

—Whaaaat?

But because it caused her anxiety, we got her a mail-in ballot, which she signed, and we posted, using two stamps, each one a couple of pennies shy of the new postal charge. Didn't we have a two-cent stamp? she asked. Wasn't it a waste to use two stamps? Wasn't anyone going to the post office?

"Nana, this could be our first black president. Let's just spring for the forty cents."

She laughed and shook her head. "I guess this is history!"

The two-stamps narrative proved important, because it marked the mail-in ballot, which she was inclined to forget, since it didn't feel like having voted. Except for the stamps.

Nana was having a hard time with the oxygen. It was important to make sure that she kept the oxygen cannulas in her nose and wrapped over her ears. She was becoming more accustomed to it, but still wanted the freedom of doing without. Sometimes Nana was convinced that she only needed it when she noticed shortness of breath. So when Karline or Gertrude left the room for a few minutes, she'd take off the cannula while watching TV. She also wished, understandably, to sleep unencumbered by the tubes. But more and more we were finding that if we let her sleep without the extra oxygen, she'd awaken sluggishly or off-balance emotionally: irritable, usually, or anxious.

After the opening concerts and school events, with the erecting and breaking down of the party tents at the headmaster's house next door, the autumnal equinox came and went, and the days began to shorten. Nana seemed afraid, and I was, too.

Chapter 19

The next week, on the afternoon Hannibal was scheduled to give a workshop to explain his process of writing the text and music, I received an urgent call on my cell from Gertrude. She said that I needed to come home as quickly as possible.

"The nurse is here, and your Nana's very upset. She's calling your name."

I could hear her in the background, shouting, as she had the Night of the Bee, and a few other times of extreme agitation.

"Can you come home?"

Our programs manager, Tarana Burke, had been hired just a couple of weeks before. Americans now know her as the creator of #MeToo, but in that moment, she was a young woman in a brand-new job assisting in the management of a small staff coordinating three concerts in two days with musicians, elected officials, three choirs, three locations, several schools, board members, and caterers. At the door to the lecture room at the University of Penn, I explained to her and to Hannibal that I'd have to leave. In fact, the workshop and reception were planned to the last detail, and they would go well.

Not so the scene at home.

It was a deep gold-and-red afternoon, just waiting to engage the long autumnal twilight. I opened the front door and heard Nana's hoarse voice. She called my name in an exhausted, yet enraged, three-note pattern she'd kept up the whole time since Gertrude's call, and my escape from the workshop and speed-limit-defying drive across the Schuylkill River to East Falls. In between her cries, the muted women's voices spoke superhuman patience and calm.

"Here she comes. You see, we told you she was on her way."

At the landing I stopped before climbing the three steps to her hallway. I was looking at a scene I could not take in.

The second-floor landing was its own wide-open room, with three windows behind me and a twelve-foot-wide, floor-to-ceiling mirror opposite. Light bounced back and forth on this landing, as did the energy of ancestors calling Nana, according to our sage-burning friend. However much I told myself that I did not take any of the spirit-talk literally, it lived for me on this wide-open landing. On either side of the mirror were doors, one to our office, and one to Nana's room. Gertrude stood in the doorframe still holding the phone she'd used to ring me. Nana perched on her wheelchair, dressed, and wearing a hastily thrown-on sweater or a jacket, not at all like Gertrude normally dressed her. She was wearing also one untied shoe over a knee-high stocking bunched at her ankle. The other shoe lay off to the side. Nurse Barbara sat on the floor in front of Nana's wheelchair, where Nana believed she had immobilized Barbara by grabbing her hands, fingers splayed, and twisting them, cross-armed. Nana grimaced. Her fear bounced off the mirror and reflected off every surface.

"Nana, Nana." I remember saying this and walking to her to touch her hands to let go of Barbara. "Where were you going?"

It was a ridiculous question. I have forgotten her precise answer. Instead I heard a female-voiced chorus, answers laid on top of each other, different words and understandings of what was happening at the moment to one centenarian whose heart was no longer getting enough oxygen to her brain.

Barbara whispered that she'd wait for me downstairs. Nana explained then with some exasperation that she refused to be dictated to or treated like a child, and that she had definitely been on her way out. I reminded her of the three steps down before the landing.

"The stair rail is there for you, but usually someone folds the seat down for you."

"I know that!"

"Okay. It's the kind of thing you can forget if you hurry."

"Don't you think I know that?"

But since I was home, and promised not to go out again that evening, she could relax now, take off her clothes, and settle down. Gertrude could put the oxygen back on—very important, especially since she'd been wrestling with someone half her age—and I'd bring up tea for us and Gertrude could get going over the bridge.

I walked Nurse Barbara out to her car and apologized. Yellow chrysanthemums cheered the threatening sky. Barbara lifted her head as if to catch a scent. No apology was necessary, she said. She had not pulled away, because she didn't want to upset Nana more—or hurt her. Despite Nana's amazing strength—she'd been holding Barbara for at least half an hour when I arrived—her heart was failing, and Barbara thought that somewhere inside, Nana sensed it. Sometimes people dropped clothing as a way to say that they needed to slough off the body they were wrapped in; sometimes they put on their shoes or coat and hat to say that they needed to leave this place.

I told Barbara that Nana did not live in the gospel-song universe where folks happily sang of "going up yonder to be with my Lord."

Still, winter was coming.

"Winter is hard," Barbara said. "Sometimes they just can't face another winter."

As if to make the point, the wind whipped Barbara's hair into her face. She held it back with one hand while the two of us turned our backs to keep dust out of our eyes. Dead leaves flew around our ankles.

No wonder Christmas came in winter, and even before it, in just a few Sundays, the season of Advent, when we start the church year waiting for the child to be born. A few yards from us was the hidden corner where the children and I buried banners decorated with Alleluias on Ash Wednesday, after which the happy word of praise is not said until Easter, when we'd dig them up with shouts of laughter. Right here in the driveway we had written prayers in chalk to memorize them. At the rocks lining the driveway we had scattered seeds as Jesus said in his Parable of the Sower, and afterward, when we read in Luke and I asked about throwing the seeds onto rock, one of the children had said: "Sometimes our minds are like rocks!" For now, we waited out the end of the church's Ordinary Time commemorating when Jesus walked among us.

I asked Barbara what we could do about Nana's increasing anxiety. She said she'd consult the geriatric psychiatrist as soon as she left us. Because Nana was suspicious of any new pills, Barbara was thinking specifically about a product they had for people who could not swallow: an antipsychotic in gel form to rub into the skin at pulse points, where it would be absorbed into the bloodstream.

When Gertrude left, she, too, said that, from her experience, Nana was feeling the end approaching. It was only normal to be afraid. But Nana had beaten it back so many times. No wonder she couldn't believe it herself. We couldn't believe it. We had a sad laugh together before Gertrude made her way into rush hour.

◦⁓◦

"Why am I still here?"

That night Nana shouted the phrase she occasionally asked of the universe and beat her fists against the mattress. Theoretically, Nana had been hoping all along for Will Hagans's perfect death. Old age without infirmity, and then one day, he had his supper, washed his teeth, as Nana would say, went to bed and simply didn't wake up. But it was a hard damn thing for death to sneak up on Nana. She was watching. When I left her at night, I saw she had one eye open, just a crack, eyebrows furrowed. She said we took too good care of her; and it was hard to die when you felt loved, she told me. But, real talk? Nana's consciousness had strapped onto her own younger self, the part who'd been on guard ever since her mother had left, lashed up in the Crow's Nest in case the Land of the Dead appeared, because she did not really intend to go ashore.

This time I patted her hand without answering. She wasn't really asking.

Chapter 20

Later that week, or maybe it was the beginning of the next, I came home from work and Gertrude's round face was glowing. She and Nana were sitting close together as an orange sun set into the warm room. Nana purred uncharacteristically. In response to my tense, questioning look, Gertrude smiled to reassure me that after the last days of tantrums, Nana was finally moving toward acceptance, rather than terrified denial, of her fast-approaching end.

Earlier that day Gertrude had allowed as how, after Nana died, she'd love to have the miniature white vendor's cart that stood thigh-high in Nana's vestibule. How they had come to this subject, I had no idea. Every single person in our circle knew Nana did not like to talk about her death or her things, or what would happen to her things after her death, except to ask me to care for them as lovingly as she had, which was impossible.

Nana's empty house still felt like the chains of Marley's ghost thrown over my shoulders, despite Laura's having lived there and taken care of things for as long as she could stand—until, in fact, it became clear that she couldn't keep it up: the long days at work, her dog alone, a lawn to rake and mow, sidewalks to shovel, suspicious neighbors. On the days when the ancient garage door wouldn't close or she rushed out and forgot to lock something, she'd spend the day at work terrified. We needed to let Laura out of the suburban house-sitting gig and back to an appropriate twenty-something life of her own choosing. I'd rather worry about Nana's things than worry about our daughter's safety.

Gertrude shared Nana's delight in her furnishings: the Chinese jardinières and blue-and-white garden stool, the coffee table books and *National Geographic* magazines, the cranberry-glass lusters on the server in the dining room. Then, they'd zeroed in on the particular white vendor's cart that sat in the vestibule, and how, in the cool months, say, right about now, Nana would begin to stock it with fruit. When you stepped in, the vestibule smelled like apples. Gertrude had just the place for it.

Evidently, they talked about it for a long time that afternoon, and about the old days, back in New Jersey, when my grandmother was in charge of herself, when she and Pop went on trips, when she made Sunday supper for the family who came to visit, bringing children, and then those children grew up and brought their own children. My goodness.

I felt my stomach cramp. It had been a festival of loss. Beautiful, yes. Tender, yes, but the analog equivalent of the movie montage at the funeral that could land you in a crying jag for the rest of the night.

After Gertrude left, Nana withdrew into herself. By the time I'd made supper and helped her to the stair rail to come down and eat with us, her face was set into the familiar hurt-

and-angry mask; and the voice that escaped her tight lips broke hard and cold in the quiet room, like china tea things left out in the weather. Gertrude, she said, seemed a little too eager to get her hands on Nana's things.

The panic I felt was selfish. Nana's presence and her escalating needs had upended our family. The schedule was relentless. As a clergy family we lived next door to the church, and now, in the rectory, we lived down the hall from Nana. When we thought she was okay for an hour, Nana would take off her headphones, sit in bed, and turn the television to maximum volume, say, to enjoy *Lawrence Welk*— "Oh, honey, is that too loud? I thought I had it quiet." There was nowhere to escape to be alone or alone together. Gertrude's three-day job with us anchored the nursing schedule. Karline was also excellent, but to find her we'd gone through a dozen trials, all with bad outcomes. Really bad.

"Oh, Nana," I said. "No. Not Gertrude. No, no, no."

Nana reminded me how I'd always liked to think the best of people, and that was nice, but I could afford to. In fact, she said, and she didn't mean to belittle me, but I could be naïve. She, on the other hand, at her age, and with the fix she was in, which is how she referred to impending mortality, she knew better.

Sometimes, when Nana started to brood, I could pull her back, or my sister could, or our daughters, or some distraction, say, how "our young man" was doing as election loomed.

"Gertrude has been so good to you, Nana."

I said it at dinner. Recognizing immediately the danger, my husband and daughter agreed.

"She loves you, Nana!"

"Do you think she wants to hurt you to get that little white cart!"

The absurdity made me giddy, but we'd lost. I knew it. Might as well have stepped into the scene in *My Fair Lady* where Eliza Doolittle, with fanciful, ungrammatical paranoia, blames relatives for the death of a sick—but strong— old woman: "Them she lived with would'ave killed her for a *hatpin*, let alone a hat!"

After we assured Nana that Karline was safe and would come the next day to take good care of her, just like always, and not kill her when I went to work, I called and had a conversation with a tearful Gertrude. Bob sat next to me. "She's been so good to Nana," he said.

Gertrude rang every few days to check on Nana.

Barbara came to the door each week and talked with us. She offered to send a new nurse, but I told her that I valued her experience with us.

We explained to Karline what had happened. She took a deep breath and smiled. Her insistence on cheer, like Gertrude's, reminded me of the Pauline call to pray without ceasing—and even more, as my husband has reminded me, the Franciscan call to make that unceasing prayer wordless, if possible. Live it: cultivate joy, thanksgiving, and empathy right where you are. Their cheerfulness acted as a prophylactic—like oxygen in tubes for someone who cannot breathe in or out fully. I wasn't sure whether Nana could breathe them in deeply enough, but I reminded myself, as I peeled out of the rectory driveway, that I could.

But what would we do without Gertrude, who loved my grandmother, as she often said, like her own mother? Smiling Gertrude, seventy years old, who'd ratcheted up her courage three times a week to drive over the bridge from New Jersey. Plump Gertrude, with her own knee pain, who made Nana's breakfast, and happily rode it to her, tray on her lap, on the stair-rail chair? Gertrude, who'd never, ever wished anyone ill?

Art Sanctuary's tenth-anniversary gala weekend was less than two weeks away, I'd caught a cold, and I was late again. In five minutes my cell phone rang. It was Karline.

When I returned, Nana was shouting my name, as before. This time, though, she had crouched at the top of her bed, one leg folded under her with the flexibility of a yogi. Still she seemed less in control of herself than I'd ever seen her. The oxygen cannula, discarded, breathed onto the floor. And, it being first thing, she'd had no food or drink. Nana squinted at me as I came into the room, still shouting my name. Her glasses lay on the night table.

"It's me, Nana." Her earphones hung on the bedrail.

"I can't HEAR you!" She sang it out, as children yell over each other in speak-to-the-hand arguments.

I approached the bed so that she could see and hear me. When I got close she lunged at me and grabbed my hands, presumably as she had Barbara's, and twisted our arms. She craned her neck, birdlike, back and forth, as if trying to discern who I might be, really.

"It's me, Nana." Even now, I recognize that I needed to say it once more, even though it would not get through.

Karline stood nearby, watching the scene that she'd hoped to avoid. But none of this was about us. I told myself this to snuff out the flame of indignation that shot up inside me as she wrenched and twisted, thinking that she had over-powered me. Karline ran across the driveway to church to get Bob, whose baritone Nana could hear without her earphones. While the two of us were alone together, she made "aargh" sounds. Her head swiveled back and forth, watching that I didn't slip or pull away, and also looking over her shoulder, as if someone were trying to sneak up behind her. I did not speak. I was stiff from leaning in an awkward position, and angry.

"Nana," Bob said as he came in, "why are you holding Lorene like that?"

She recognized his voice and softened as he spoke.

"Tell 'er I'll make her a cup of coffee," I muttered to him, irritably.

Bob talked her down from the ledge of suspicion—enough, at least, to let go of my hands. I did go downstairs to make coffee, resenting how each of us—Gertrude, too, poor thing—had learned to make this particular bad cup of coffee exactly as she liked it: just this much of this one brand of instant, one sugar, half a Splenda, just this much half-and-half to make it Peruvian brown, and to do it fast so that it was just hot enough to slurp for a taste, and then could wait through half of breakfast and still be very, very warm. We all knuckled to it.

I tried to remind myself that she had remembered every single preference of mine she could know for fifty years, from the texture of oatmeal to the pear nectar she sent me in boarding school, despite the postage costing more than the drink.

Instead I rang the office to say that I was trapped in elder-care world and would call back in an hour.

Back upstairs, Karline and Bob had made some progress. Nana was wearing her bathrobe and glasses, but not the cannula. Karline had set up her TV table in front of her, and she was sitting on the side of the bed, waiting.

I put down a napkin and the cup, hoping for the caffeine and sugar to hit her bloodstream for a chemical fix, which we'd augment soon with oxygen. She put her hand into the handle, and then reached the cup toward me. Now her voice cloyed falsely: "Lorene, you've been working so hard, and you've been sick. Here. You should have some of this first; it'll make your cold feel better."

Bob and Karline and I exchanged glances. I did not know what they were thinking, but I erupted. She might be oxygen-deprived, she might have a hellhound on her trail, but I could not tolerate being told to test the coffee I'd just made as if I were trying to poison her. For the first time, I shouted at my grandmother: "You want the coffee, Nana, drink it. You don't want it, well, throw it into the pot. But I will not drink it first. I made it for you.

"You know what I'm saying, Nana? I don't play mind games. I don't give 'em, and I don't take 'em!"

The cup was still in her hand, outstretched. She put it down on the table and crumpled into herself. "Oh, honey, I'm sorry," she said. "But you don't know! The fix I'm in I can't trust the Lord Jesus Christ!"

Karline's eyes opened wide, and she stepped out of the room to make a shocked inhalation. Bob and I shared a relieved sigh. "Nana," I told her, "the fix you're in, you can't trust anybody else."

She humphed. "What does Bob say? What's going to happen to me?"

Still standing in the room behind her, Bob moved in front of her and said something to Nana about her soon "seeing God face-to-face." He phrased it in such a way as to keep it theoretical and offered to say a prayer with her.

She agreed but asked, as usual, that it not be a long one.

Then, having dispelled the hellhounds and granddaughter impersonators, Bob returned to church and Nana agreed to oxygen and breakfast.

Although I went to work that day, and Karline increased her days, I stayed home more often. Nurse Barbara sent the special gel by courier. But unlike any other woman of color I'd ever known, Nana did not need or even like skin lotions, so I had to apply it surreptitiously. A friend I had told about the difficulties of cutting Nana's toenails suggested I do her pedicures at night to relax her and rub the gel on the insides of her ankles. But Nana did not like anyone to touch her feet, and only allowed me to cut her nails when they grew long enough to cause her discomfort. So, I put the gel onto my palms when I put on her socks, since her feet were often cold; or when I held her around the rib cage to steady her to sit on the pot; or after I washed her hands and cleaned the nails.

"What's that greasy stuff I feel?"

"It's good for you. Here, I'll rub it in."

"I don't need anything on my skin . . . They're always say-ing my skin is so smooth." (This said facetiously.)

"But I'm washing your hands so much now."

"Why *do* you wash them so much?"

"Germs, germs, germs, Nana."

"Oh, Lord, don't let me get a cold. Not like I am now."

"No harm. And when I wash yours, I'm washing mine, too. Definitely no harm there."

"Because you're out in the world."

But for the time being, I went abroad virtually. The days were strange. I moved the computer into her room—did I have a laptop then, maybe? And I worked from home. I remember joking about feeling as loopy as Nana and cc'ing my staff with instructions to check me, because I was making errors and catching only some of them.

Help me, please.

During this last push to publicize our events, the chair of our board donated some hours of consultation with a black advertising executive. David Brown rang my cell phone. I was working in Nana's room while she napped, as she did more often now. David liked our marketing mate-rials and would get information to some media people who listened to him faster than to us. I thanked him, and then he told me that he was also an ordained Methodist minis-ter, and that although it seemed like I had plenty of church resources in my life, he wanted to take a moment to offer his help should I need it, and just to make a human, in addition to a professional, connection. As I did two or three times when a work connection caught me off guard with caring, I burst into tears.

Not until this past year, when I was recalling this moment to friends, did someone say: "Of course you were washing that gel off your hands, right?"

No. Not once. It never occurred to me.

I remember the day that the dog took up residence in Nana's room. Angus was our second Border terrier, nowhere as dear as our first, Rosie, or our current one, Gracie, and definitely not a fan of the rectory open-door protocol. Maybe we should have given him a name that ended in a happy, long $\bar{e}$ sound. I tried Harry, but nobody would go for it. Bob had discovered the breed researching possibilities to help us rid our basement of rat traffic during construction on our block; a pre-seminary profile for *The New Yorker*, "Rat Catcher," had taken him to Caithness, Scotland, to interview a man who had raised terriers and other dogs to hunt. It sounded like the end of the world where everything was wild and rough: the landscape, the dog trainer, the dogs themselves.

Angus was chuff-chuff brusque, combative as befits a breed meant to run after big lurchers over miles of heath, and then finish the hunt by pulling badgers out of their own holes. He took Gertrude and Karline as family members who needed to be protected along with Nana. I don't think he was a great fan of Christianity. Although, because it was the family business, as Zoë said, he tried to tolerate the parishioners coming and going. He liked mass in the house better than vestry meetings, and adults better than children. He jumped up and nipped my nephew on the forehead when he, his little brother, and my sister came down on a mercy visit, prompting a parish-wide discussion by everyone who'd ever had a dog who'd bitten someone. I ordered a shock collar for Angus. But the fact is, when Nana's immune system began to fail, Angus knew it first and began his vigil.

Since then, medical researchers have begun to investigate animals' ability to sense illness. Right about when Angus claimed Nana's couch—a cheeky canine first that we decided to let slide—*The New England Journal of Medicine* published the story of Oscar, the death cat. Oscar had been adopted by the nursing staff in a Rhode Island nursing home. As he grew to cathood, Oscar began to sniff the hallways. He'd find a particular patient and curl up next to him or her. The patient thus indicated would inevitably die soon thereafter. Oscar's warning gave the staff a signal to call the family. Doctors interpreted Oscar's behavior as akin to current death-predictive algorithms.

Hospice might see Oscar's as a different vocation. Maybe he understood himself to be a chaplain. Maybe he understood that his new home needed someone to express consolation by pressing soft, warm-blooded courage against frightened, cooling limbs. As oral history confirms, Oscar was not the only animal to use his body as a compact "ministry of presence." Bob was given the concept in seminary. It was a great help for clergy who are called to stand with people in extreme moments of their lives when words are inadequate. Seminary professors and thousands of years of human experience know that ideologies and theories, even faith itself, can fail, but that the presence of another human being keeps us, at least, from being alone. The ministry of it, it seemed to me when Bob explained it, was to hold one's entire self present, mentally and emotionally available as people's pain and confusion and fear rolls over and through them. The clergy must be anchored enough to take it— without being overwhelmed by excruciating empathy.

I think that Oscar chose his vocation, because on the day Nana was napping, and I was bawling on the phone with David, and likely whacko from the medicinal gel, I watched Angus choose his.

Chapter 21

Carole and her two young sons, Joshua and Coleman, came on one of those weekends. No doubt I had called and complained. I was losing capacity. In preparation for their visit Nana let me try to scrub the dandruff scales that were forming on her scalp. A day or two before, Nana asked Karline to do special sprucing in her room. We piled in extra logs and I lay newspaper and kindling ready for the match. Nana delightedly sampled a carton of the chocolate milk I bought for the boys and we talked about what to have ready for them to eat when they came—although my sister often brought dinner in shopping bags plus treats that lasted for days.

On some trips, Michael came, too. Carole's husband, an investment banker who had taught me how to manage Art Sanctuary's money, and had served as treasurer on the board, was the other man in Nana's life. She admired his devotion to the family, as she liked to say, and his professional success. Whenever they visited, it was a party. It was the family coming to dinner again, like the old days. Nana's heart perked up and pumped color back into her face against one of the fresh L.L.Bean nightgowns I'd bought the year before, but that she'd been saving. ("Saving for what, Nana?")

Their SUV would zip up the drive, as fast as I drove our car, if Carole were driving, sedately if it were Michael, and the dog would bark, and we'd open the door to the nephews who tumbled into the house with pre-K life and energy, language like song, bodies dancing. Michael would come carrying bags, and Carole would trail them, a beautiful, compact woman, body slung with bags of food and presents for everyone. Zoë and Bob would help with the bags, and she and I would come after, connecting fast-fast. Because the boys were still young, Carole did not fly for an airline, but rather gave private lessons, took short stints for a celeb or two, and worked in simulators. She volunteered with the Organization of Black American Pilots and has a goal to get a hundred young black women up into the sky with her. That would more than double the number of black women commercial pilots flying in the United States today. We'd follow the tiny crowd of our family, grinning at our shared exhaustion as if to stare it down, and Carole would ask her signature laugh line, "Why are we like this? What did they do to us?" at which point we'd double over for a moment of sibling hilarity before coming into the house to the children, husbands, and elderly grandmother.

Was it this trip or another one when Nana shook her bell for twenty seconds as a joke to indicate that everyone was downstairs bonding and leaving her alone? Did Carole ask me again on this trip what we had been thinking to give Nana a bell, even as Zoë shook her head and the boys clambered up the stairs to see.

"She likes her bell." That would be Bob.

Was this the visit when Dad came, too, and the boys climbed over him happily? Or was it the time when Zoë watched *The Incredibles* with Joshua and Coleman before they could say *r*'s, and renaming it *The Inkedibles* for us ever after? Was it this visit when Bob and I drove out for what our family had come to call a Russian picnic: cold food and hot coffee to enjoy in winter weather when the brown-and-green fields outside the city lay open and quiet?

For sure, it was Nana's last, best at-home, and a beautiful picture I keep in mind: I'm looking into the room after coming home and seeing Carole perched on the bed, Nana animated, my nephews playing on the floor, their usual rough-and-tumble gentled by the close quarters and the presence of this aged relative who required special care. There's a glow, yes, rosy, because that's how it came to me, and a fermata over the door, holding the quiet rest for as long as I need to: family together at the end of one life and the beginning of others, with my sister and me and our partners holding steady in the center, because that's how memory works. When I came back to finish the evening bedtime ritual, the glow was gone.

Bedtime ritual was a euphemism. By November Nana was sleeping no more than a few hours at a time. I started to stay in the room with her and the dog until I heard her breathing steady. I'd crawl into bed with Bob, who would wake up and ask sleepy, funny questions:

"You and the dog ready for bed yet?

"Does Nana know where the car keys are?"

Now and then he'd say one of my favorite blessings: "May the Lord bless you and keep you; the Lord make his face to shine upon you, and be gracious unto you; the Lord lift up his countenance upon you, and give you peace."

I liked to think of peace and try to pull it into me, just as Bob folded me into the warmth of his body. As in labor, we began to pay stricter attention to the moments of rest. Nana would be up again in a few hours.

One night I fell asleep on the toilet with the door open to her room so I could hear her. I was confused when I heard her shouting that her leg was stuck in the slat of the bed, which I'd raised after she fell a few nights earlier either going to the potty or bypassing it altogether.

"Hang on, Nana!"

How could I shout loudly enough so that she could hear me without waking Bob and Zoë?

Calling and wrenching. One cellulite-free leg protruded through the bed rail. I was washing my hands fast. "Coming, coming, coming."

She couldn't hear me. Why say it?

"I'm stuck in this thing!" She rattled the metal bed.

Terrified that she would break her hip, I touched her leg and shoulder at once. "Nana! Just a minute, please. Let me see how to get you unstuck."

"I know I'm stuck."

"Please stop pushing."

Finally, she submitted to lying down and letting me roll

her away from the bed rail to free the leg and put down the rail. The exertion, however, had proved too much for her bladder. The bed was wet.

"Come on," I said, "if you sit here on the potty chair, I can change the bed."

Nana asked for a basin of soapy water to wash herself while I made the bed. Irritated at having to stop, I got the basin, set it up on the folding table, put a washcloth in and a towel next to it. I took her right hand and ran them over the toilette items so she could feel where they were. I kept the room dark so that our bodies would remember it was night-time. Both of us were inclined these days to wake up and fuss. Besides, her vision was so minimal that she did most things by habit and feel.

We moved to the sound of water and cotton. I thought the movements were soothing.

I helped her into a fresh nightgown. Pivot. Sat back onto the bed. What was supposed to happen was that she'd lie down on the tight, fragrant bedclothes, snuggle into the mommy blanket, blessedly still dry, and, comforted, relax into the breeze of the fan at the foot of the bed.

Instead, still stiffened with the same energy that had poked her leg through the rail, she sat straight and white against the night light and said: "I'll never get back to sleep."

"Oh, Jesus, Nana. Well, I will. We have got to sleep."

Then she looked at me, her eyes dark in the nearly skeletal face: "You wish I was dead. I know it!"

I moved back to sidestep spittle.

"You want me dead. Don't you?"

Now it was raw biology, generations competing: her care

217

vs. my sleep. If she didn't get care, she'd die; and if I didn't get sleep, I'd . . . what? Reach the end of love? Find that my love for her was as conditional as I found hers had been for us? Would I begrudge her this essential sharing of life's energy? Would I find myself tempted to betray love itself, as sacred and as regular as air and water, God in the breath of life? Without sleep, how could I stay in the cave of her room, once an elegant parlor, now some transitional place between life and death, and spin straw into gold. I needed sleep to knit up the ragged ends of rage, of not getting my own, of never being enough to satisfy her, as I felt I hadn't satisfied my parents, and ancestors who demanded redemption through their offspring.

She had called me out all right.

I couldn't answer.

It was early morning, the witching hour to be sure, when she gave and demanded a raw, sometimes ugly honesty.

"Don't you?"

I leaned over and hissed into her ear: "You are shouting, Nana, and I have been trying to empty the bucket. I cannot shout back. The family is asleep!"

"Oh." A swallowed syllable followed me to the adjoining bathroom, showing me that she still had breeding and courtesy, as if the yelling to awaken us all at night never happened.

Of course, part of me did want her dead. I wanted a full night's sleep without worrying about the next crisis, the next stinkbug that she'd swear was a bee, which she knew and we didn't, that would sting and sting and sting her when she lay alone and vulnerable. I wanted her to take with her the demons that trailed behind her, outside the windows, in the trees, lighting up the landing and bouncing back and forth between the mirror and the windows where the chair rail landed.

Yes. I wanted to stop the collapse of the Nana I'd known into this person, whom I recognized, and had been a fool not to notice before, back when she had more flesh to hide the bones, and courtesy and material health to hide the fear in her heart. That heart! So many demands now, as it tried to pump blood through muscle and past bone that remembered all the times over a century when she had called for God, who had no more answered than her mother, dead when she was six. And so her heart pumped through the closed loop of remembered rage, no choice but to lash out against and then withdraw from anyone who did not love her perfectly.

And, from Lizzie on through an entire century, none of us had.

So, yes, I did want her dead, even though after she died, I stored the grief in my muscles and in my fat cells and in the marrow of my bones and in the joints, where I could not reach it, and where, if I did more and more service for children, for black people, I could keep it, mostly undisturbed, like crystals in the joints, like liquid in a cyst that will not be absorbed.

"We know it's coming, Nana." I said it close to her, so that she could hear me without the constant unintended emphasis of shouting. "We both know that. But, listen, hey, you're still here, I'm still here, how about a snack?"

By now, Nana was sitting up in bed, her flexible legs bent under the covers. "Well," she pondered, "I know this might sound funny coming from someone so close to death, but . . ."

"You wanna know what's in the fridge?"

She laughed her hollow laugh. "One of those fancy tarts?"

"With the fruit?"

"Do we have any more of those?"

"I think so. Lemme see."

When I returned, we arranged ourselves around the tea table and tucked into a substantial low tea. The small light on the night table was on. I can still see it behind her head.

"Now, honey," Nana said, nice and easy like old times, "I have one favor to ask. Would you do something for me?"

"I don't know, Nana. Depends what it is."

"Now don't be difficult."

"What's the favor, Nana?"

"So you'll agree to do it for me?"

"Not before I know what it is."

"Well, you know I want to be cremated."

"Yep."

"Okay. Now I want you to find where my father is buried—"

"Just tell me, Nana. Where is he buried?"

"I took you."

"I don't remember."

"I'm sure I took you."

"Not since I can remember. Do you know the name?"

"Eden, I think. You father will know. We have a family plot."

"Okay, Nana. I'll ask Daddy. And we'll find the family plot—"

"Now I want you to get a small shovel and take my ashes. You may have to go at night. And I want you to dig a hole and pour it in. All right?"

"Oh, for God's sake!"

"What?"

"No, Nana."

"Why not?"

We went on this way for a while, my arguing that the only service a cemetery has to sell is opening plots and burying people, and that digging a hole would be akin to theft. Plus, it would put the kibosh on a church service, and keep other loved ones from having a moment together to express their love and grief.

Nana grunted. I remembered Pop-Pop.

Nana allowed as how she would never be able to get to sleep. I countered that sleep did not depend on bending other people to one's will. She said that I could make words mean anything I wanted. We chatted on like that, as if we were improvising for an end-of-life French farce, until finally she told me to go to my own bed with my husband. Her speech was a little slurred.

To distract us both, I told her that I'd remembered the sequence for "The Old Lady and Her Pig."

"Who got it going? It was the butcher, wasn't it?"

"No, I thought so, but I looked it up."

"Well, who was it?"

"Ready?" I rolled her into bed, but left on the earphones just long enough for her to hear the whole line, spread out across the English countryside we used to imagine: "You have to give hay to the cow before she will give you a bowl of milk; and you have to give the cat a bowl of milk before she's willing to do her part."

"Oh, that's right! The rat. What does the rat do?"

I made a big inhale sound, like she used to do before saying the whole list with deadly percussion: "Soooo the cat began to kill the rat; the rat began to gnaw the rope; the rope began to hang the butcher; the butcher began to kill the ox; the ox began to drink the water; the water began to quench the fire; the fire began to burn the stick; the stick began to beat the dog; the dog began to bite the pig; the little pig in a fright jumped over the stile; and so the old woman got home that night.

"How's that for a peaceful good night?"

Nana laughed. She ignored or did not hear my sarcasm. "Nice."

Downstairs, predawn, in the kitchen as I washed the tea things, I began to run through the Art Sanctuary schedule for the next two weeks, but my mind was so foggy I kept getting details wrong. Pickups and drop-offs and tech and brochures and payments; all muddled.

So I called the on-call nurse at Holy Redeemer and asked her to explain Family Respite care to me again. She said they'd take your loved one in for five days, although for the first three you were not allowed to call, in order to let them get situated.

"Like summer camp."

"Exactly!" Cheerful, the nurse told me that residents

often appreciated a change of scene themselves. Nana would probably thank us for this.

"No," I said, "she won't. Nana's narrative is that at the end, everybody takes care of himself, and that everyone and anyone is liable to abandon her. And this will prove her right."

My internal Key-and-Peele Anger Translator asked me: *Like who died and left you God? She's still up there trying to think of a way to get back to New Jersey. And you think you're taking care of her? You was 'sleep on the john long enough to let her get herself into the medical bed-rail jaws of death, surefire old-people hip-cracking position. No, baby, you are no longer taking good care of shit.*

The nurse on call was listening in.

"She'll hate us for it," I said, more to myself than to her. "But I have to do it anyway."

Push had come to shove, and I'd chosen me and mine over her. This is what Nana had been telling me I'd do. For years.

The nurse said they'd call me when they had an available bed.

Chapter 22

Holy Redeemer did not call for a week, so Karline agreed to work through the tenth-anniversary weekend. Laura said she would come at night, although I hesitated to tell her that I was sleeping most of the night on Nana's couch with Angus. One other nurse whom Nana delighted in, for the moment, said she'd be on call. She'd spent the night once that week, but when I woke as I did now two or three times a night, and walked past Nana's door to the bathroom, I saw that she was tucked in so tightly that she could not get out of bed at all, which looked to me like one half step down from restraints. Holy Redeemer promised no restraints. For the weekend coming, we had Plan Bs, and a Plan C we hoped not to have to use. She wasn't going to like them.

My mother called to check on us and offered to come stay if necessary. "Mom and I know each other," she said.

Plan D: *Family Feud: The Reality Show.*

"Thanks, Mom."

"I know that's not what you want, but if you need a hand—that's all I'm saying."

Not for the first time, we referenced Zoë's Chinese

fairy tale book where people migrating from one region to another as the Yellow River flooded carried their grandparents piggyback across the mountains. She had the flexibility still . . .

Like family, the hospice facility rang very, very early on Friday. They had a bed; if we wanted it, they would send an ambulance for Nana midmorning.

From here, memory shoots through like lightning, illuminating moments:

I hear Carole's voice. It was at once my little sister's, coffee-creamy smooth, and also airplane-pilot precise, aggressive, can-do. She whose birth I had awaited in the nook off Nana's kitchen by the dial telephone when I was seven; she who had shared the delight of those sage-green weekends that smelled of yew bushes and rotisserie chicken, Downy, and sunshine. Carole had looked at me with tears in her shiny eyes when my parents' separation opened up the poisonous underground seam of divorce rage that had burned in Nana since the 1940s. We'd held hands walking into her house those first lonely Christmases when Nana laid out presents and then shut herself down.

"Do you need me to be there?" Carole asked me.

"Yes, please."

God knew I needed her. I needed Nana to know there was no appeal. I needed help putting her into an ambulance and sending her off. I needed Carole to remember it with me. I needed not to be alone with lonely Nana facing lonely ejection from the house she'd entered reluctantly a year and a half ago thinking it would be six weeks. I needed Carole to forgive me.

She'd get the boys off to school, she said, and come directly.

I feel Bob's body just as it was then, holding me before I told Zoë and watched her early morning eyes come to attention behind her glasses.

I feel the sense of betrayal as I watched Nana eat her breakfast. As always she saved a piece of sausage just the size of the tip of her pinkie finger and held it down for Angus, who lay waiting at her feet and took if from her with accustomed delicacy.

I see myself making a list so as to make one phone call to the Art Sanctuary staff, not several anxiety-producing crazy-boss calls, but by this time, and with my having been in and out for weeks, they had the event planned to run just fine without me. I thought of it as a metaphor for death. I found myself talking to Bob about coming in at the middle of the movie and going out while it's still playing. Hannibal and the West Philly choir and the television anchor were prepared. The school auditorium was ready. Tech. Check. No buses drama.

Carole arrived ready to do what had to be done.

The drivers steered the boxy ambulance up the tricky

driveway. Low branches of the Japanese maple scraped the sides. When I heard them screech like nails on a chalkboard, I told Nana what was about to happen. She looked to Carole, realizing with what looked like slow-motion panic why Carole was here on a weekday morning. Carole said something to her. We asked the guys to wait a moment so we could do this gently. She was closer to death than when we did this at her house, but I wondered how much closer.

And now, like soldiers recounting a moment they don't remember so much as drop into, the story becomes a waking dream:

This ambulance company's special gurney is more like a narrow bed than a slab. That's good, I think. They've brought a canister of oxygen upstairs with them. Very good. They unhook her cannula from the machine under the window and transfer it to the tank, which can nestle behind her legs. It's cold, though, and she moans. They ask for something to keep it from touching her legs. Carole finds the perfect blue-and-white blanket folded on the shelf in Nana's closet. It's from the *b'nai mitzvah* of Zoë's classmates and bears their names, Emily and Adam, and the date of the occasion. (At Holy Redeemer, the Jewish family counselor will wonder whether we've wrapped her in it to let caretakers know she is Jewish, or maybe to assure her.)

Meanwhile, Nana is talking. She says, "Oh, no. Don't do this." She says, "I won't be here long. Just let me stay." She says, "I'm just trying to die," which will haunt my sister for years. She grabs my collar and cries my name. The name she chose because she did not like Rosalie.

As I suspected, the ambulance has trouble with the last

turn out of the driveway, but one gets out and leads the other.
They do not jostle Nana by rolling over the boulders on the
church side, and they do not rip branches from the Japanese
maple like the trucks that brought the voting machines.

Carole and I hugged. We joked that Nana'd be back before
we know it, and she probably wouldn't, but it wasn't impossible, and then both of us began to cry. We cried as we drove,
Carole north on the New Jersey Turnpike to her children, me
on the road west to the High School of the Future.

At the school, the buses and cars had already parked and
emptied. I sat in the car for a few minutes trying to shed my
feeling of betrayal and get myself together for the rest of the
day. I kept seeing in my mind Nana's silhouette in the night,
sitting up with one leg stuck through the sides of the hospital bed. Holy Redeemer's brochures stated unequivocally
that they would not use restraints in hospice care. But what
would they do if she got up and fell? I asked myself questions
and stopped myself and asked again until I dried my face,
put on lipstick, and made myself go inside to see at least the
end of the program.

Inside, past security, I heard the young people singing,
singing, singing. Inside, the full auditorium smelled like
school: perfumes, bodies, breath. Hannibal was playing with
the choir, his body S-curved around the lungs that concen-
trated air into his battered coronet to ring golden jazz counterpoint to the kids singing his words:

> . . . *For the number is set:*
> *Each smile, each step, each tear.*

So rejoice in the gift of living one more day;
Give to life all your love before you pass away.

Rejoice, Rejoice
Rejoice, Rejoice
Rejoice, Rejoice
Rejoice, Rejoice

I sang it with them, crying freely.

That night I was glad I had. Our host for the gala got caught in traffic, and the morning matinee had drained me of tears, so that I could welcome our donor-audience dry-eyed and smiling. A full moon rose and shone on us. The adult choirs sang, Donald conducted, the soloists nailed each performance, and Hannibal and the quintet worked classical European and jazz music into American fusion in honor of Father Paul Washington nine days after the election of our first black president.

At the reception, the lead soprano at the Church of the Advocate told me she had prepared herself not to like the music. In fact, she'd been dreading the whole expensive evening. "Usually, I don't like modern music."

Then, with her face tinged blue by the lights in Girard College's marble Founder's Hall, she smiled thoughtfully. The music didn't talk about heaven, she said into my ear over the reception party noise; instead, it had conveyed transcendence.

On Saturday night, having succeeded so brilliantly the night before, the choir and musicians conveyed it some more. This time they were performing at the Advocate, Father Paul's church, where he had not only held public black liberation events and ordained the first women priests, but also performed Sunday mass, baptized children and married lovers and buried the dead. At once monumental and tender, the music flew around the French Gothic cathedral that was also a simple church. Coltrane had played here. Surrounded by black liberation murals and stone carvings, the musicians and the mass choir were no longer performing. Like the children from West Philly, they were testifying. The Book of Exodus says that we cannot see the face of God and live.

But we can hear it. I wished Nana could hear it, too. Her young man was in the White House and that very nice musician friend of mine was playing what she'd need to take with her, given the fix she was in. I felt like she'd dragged our ancestors into the rectory with us, and the music let us bring them to church to set them free.

What was Nana hearing now? The gentle young men had put aside her earphones and glasses. Like those novels about the rapture. Like she didn't need them anymore.

On Monday Bob drove us to the hospice wing of Holy Redeemer's sprawling medical campus outside Philadelphia. The reception nurse led us to a family waiting room. It was modest and private. We waited while they brought her. She was dressed in warmer, comfier clothes than hospitals usually provide. Without glasses, earphones, or oxygen, she looked vulnerable, more like herself. I came close so she could hear me.

"Nana," I said, still dreading the response I knew was coming, "it's Lorene. And Bob's here, too. We've come to see how you're doing."

She looked at my face, close to hers now. The anxiety mask was gone. Somehow the geriatric psychiatrist had found exactly the medication cocktail to soothe Nana's fear and return her to herself. With muscles at rest, her face could now register several emotions in a row: confusion, disbelief, surprise. She looked back and forth between us to confirm, and then reached around my neck and pulled me to her.

"Oh, honey," she said, "I was afraid you'd never find me. You won't believe where I've been."

Then, for the first time since she began this last leg of her life, Nana herself cried.

Chapter 23

Nana Jackson didn't ask to return to the rectory; we didn't offer. She'd enjoyed her sit-in showers, the nurse assured me. Her hair had been washed, and the scales on her scalp were gone. For a couple more evenings, when we drove to Holy Redeemer, we'd find her near the nurses' station where people came and went. She'd be sitting in a big recliner with wheels that could be rolled through the hallways and to her room.

She did not care to watch television anymore. Although she could still say words, she seldom spoke. It was as if she was no longer interested in worrying about the things of this world. I wheeled her up and down the short hall in her puffy recliner. Or we'd pause in the empty sunroom. She liked a sherbet they stocked in little paper cups, and they'd bring it to me to feed her when they thought she might eat some spoonfuls.

Within a few nights, she was in bed when we came and didn't get up again.

Nine days after Nana arrived, on a Sunday morning, the hospice nurse rang to say Nana had begun "actively dying."

I called a Sunday school mother to substitute for me at church. She and her family swept across the driveway as we were leaving, arms open to reassure us.

I went first; Bob presided over the service and came soon after. Bob, Laura, Zoë, and I stood and sat around Nana. She'd stopped talking altogether, and her eyes were mostly closed. We put to Nana's lips a quarter teaspoon of the sherbet she'd favored the past week. Then, just a moistened swab. Or daubed her forehead and cheeks with a cool cloth.

"Not too much." We quoted her to each other. Not too much: touching, fussing, oil, affection, God-talk, death-talk, food.

My dad came, and Bob and the girls went to get us lunch. Dad looked at Nana, patted her arm, and looked away. Two Sundays before we set them up to have dinner in her room, just the two of them, while we ate downstairs. What had they talked about? I asked. He couldn't remember, but it was their last supper. Dad, too, referenced his grandfather's easy death in his sleep. Understandably. Nana's death was hard. Her chest and back and belly all contracted and expanded with jerky force with each breath, time after time, breath after breath. Her lips blew in and out with the force of the life she held onto.

We talked on the phone with Carole, who was threatening to make the trip, but was away in Massachusetts, a drive that would take eight hours at best. My mother rang to check on us and urged me to dissuade Carole from making a dangerous drive by herself. We lobbed phone calls back and forth and drinks and sandwiches among those close and far while Nana's chest snatched air and her lips kept time.

Dad sat in a chair near Nana, just as he had sat near her at her office for years. Late in the afternoon he said goodbye, hugged Nana, and left. Someone walked out with him and came back, like waves. Toward evening, although it seemed like a false equivalence, Laura had to admit that her dog had been locked in Nana's house alone most of the day, and Angus had been, too, so Bob and Laura left to care for living dependents while time and life rolled past the hospice facility. They promised to return whenever we'd call.

Zoë stayed with me. We talked about death a little, the fact that Nana's limbs were shutting down, turning blue in order to save energy. I held onto Nana's cold hand.

"But then," I said to Nana, still breathing, eyes closed, "your hands are always cold."

After a while, Zoë said that she'd brought her laptop, and wondered whether we could watch something or if that would be disrespectful. Well, considering how much Nana enjoyed watching movies with them, I said, to Zoë and to Nana, I thought there'd be no harm.

Zoë always remembers the particular movie, and that she thought it may have been inappropriate to the occasion. I forget it each time, even now, after calling her and talking to her about it to collect her memories. I remember how loud the sound of Nana's breath became, dry, as if something hard were in her lungs. Hospice people floated in and out like angels, doing things they knew would help her and us.

One woman pressed her lips together and nodded. "That's the death rattle," she whispered very quietly. "You may need to give her permission to go. Some people need permission."

Zoë and I nodded appreciatively, even though we knew Nana did not want our permission. Simeon sat in the temple waiting because God had promised him that he would not die until the promised savior appeared. What was Nana waiting for? What had she been promised? What was she afraid of? After all this time together, I didn't know. But I wished I did.

Instead, I listened to that rattle in her lungs, as if something hard were forming, as if all the resentments and hurts and the bitterness were being reduced by this terrible last effort. She was her own life kiln, drying out what was left so that she could breathe it out into this room that now smelled of her death breath and of us, our living bodies that were breathing her in.

Take, breathe, this is the last bit I can squeeze from my body. This is life, just life, the fact of it like yoga says, like Hebrew says, like language and song and dreams say. Like you hear in the wind, in the trumpet. One more breath; this is time. Don't you get it? You who had asthma and thought when your lungs clamped down that you had to give up; listen to this rattling around in me still: this is life! I will wring every breath, every second. For these last moments allotted to me, heart beats, brain works, I breathe.

"Do you need our permission, Nana?"

Don't waste it. Here, save it. Put it in the fridge; I'll get to it. Can't you use it later?

The rattle became uneven. Zoë crowded in next to me and lay hands on Nana. We were tired. It was night. Bedtime. Nana had been at it all day.

"Nana, you've been so strong. Good job, Nana. You've done it."

We told her we were there. We called the family names. We told her that we loved her. We told her we'd stay with her. And we waited as the rattle went as hard as coal. Life and death banged against her ribs like a pinball, mercilessly. We told her she'd be all right. Bob's voice in my mind prayed our "sure and certain hope."

She gagged and stopped.

She snagged one more, last, hard, impossible gulping gasp.

Then nothing. The little room went silent.

I looked at Zoë. We were stunned. Dear Jesus. How could it be that Nana was gone?

Chapter 24

Nana died on November 23, six days before my birthday, which was also the first day of Advent that year. I couldn't manage to make Advent calendars for the children or have materials ready for Advent wreaths. We'd made them every year: three blue candles and one pink, to light each Sunday approaching Christmas. I couldn't find the blue candles in the basement containers and couldn't make time to go buy them; I couldn't find artificial evergreen garlands or the energy to cut boughs from the tree in the yard and twist them along hangers. "Coming" is how the church calls the Advent season. We await his coming. It's New Life, the new year beginning when Baby Jesus comes again. Just in case you wrecked last year, you get another chance. Nana wouldn't get another chance.

Dad and I drove to Eden Cemetery together in November rain because the next of kin must sign for cremation. Plus, I wanted to find the family plot where William Scarlett and Lizzie Hagans were buried so there'd be no bumbling at the funeral. On the fifty-foot walk from the car to the door of the cemetery office, the cold, gray rain found its way down our collars. On the door was a note from the volunteer office staff saying she'd be back in an hour.

"Wanna get some coffee?" I asked.

We drove back through the gray-stone entryway and tall wrought-iron gates. In 1902 Collingdale residents had blocked the entrance saying they did not want African burials in their town. But Congressman White and the others, including Will Hagans, would not take no. A little more than a century later, in the summer before Nana died, 2008, vandals broke into Eden and knocked over two hundred gravestones, including that of educator and activist Octavius Catto, who was gunned down during violence against blacks on Election Day, October 10, 1871. Eden has very little room left—and very little income. Volunteers mostly run the cemetery. It's a wonder they keep regular hours at all.

Dad and I found a Dunkin' Donuts restaurant to wait and drink coffee. I took the opportunity to talk about Nana's service: where, when, who; the burial and the reception after. I was about to tell him about the older woman on Art Sanctuary's board who used to say she did not want an "open mic funeral" where one after another "babbling grandchildren get up sniveling and saying things nobody can understand." We needed some levity, for sure, but I could see that Dad wanted to talk, too, so I shut up.

Dad had a different vision for Nana's burial, he said. The way he had been thinking—and he knew this is what she would have wanted—was to collect Nana's ashes (pause), and then come back at night with a small shovel (pause), just the two of us, find the family plot (pause), dig a hole—and pour her ashes in. He lowered his head and peered meaningfully at me for a reaction.

I blurted out a big, old, rude laugh. "Dad, that's ridiculous."

He rocked back, offended. "This was m'mother's dying wish."

"Yeah, but it's still ridiculous." My heart began to pound. With Nana dead and Mom divorced, I was next in line for separation. That's what Dad's body language seemed to say. I'd watched this face, mouth downturned into a reversed U, withdraw into itself before. Throughout my life, it had been a warning.

"This isn't like the Christmas trees, Dad."

He couldn't keep himself from smiling.

Was he imagining that we'd do this job like we used to steal trees on Christmas Eve? We'd venture out after the tree sellers had gone home and locked up. Depending on the weather that could be ten or eleven—or later, if it wasn't too cold. Dad would have been looking at potential places the week before. He'd have chosen one that looked doable. Sometimes that meant passing up lots where owners were burning their trees (on Christmas Eve, talk about Scrooges, we said!) or hoping to snag last-minute sales: people driving in from out-of-town, we figured. Dad would climb over the fence and hold up a tree he thought looked good. I'd stay outside the fence watching, a proxy for Mom. She'd have to wait up late to trim it; so we were not to come home dragging a sad piece of a Charlie Brown tree. But the places he chose had to be dark, so it was hard to see.

Every year I was afraid we'd be caught. After the big snow

when the car careened into a snowdrift and Dad had to carry me because my asthma flared, I also became afraid of the weather. We'd driven these same roads those Christmas Eves, right near Eden, evading white cops who were home behind neat little green lawns after a hard day in the red-lined Bantustans, like where I grew up.

Did Dad think that Nana's pirate burial would be a next-level Christmas tree adventure? Like some cheap hero's journey, where we'd arrive home bringing forbidden knowledge, having done what other people wished to do, but didn't dare?

He continued to smile boyish charm.

"It's gotta be illegal, Dad." I remembered having read that ashes could not be thrown within three miles of shore.

"I doubt that."

"In Pennsylvania, you can't just pour ashes into the ground. Must be some kind of rules." Turns out there aren't. But how was I letting this absurd conversation lure me into saying any old thing? This is how my parents had argued. Just one thing after another until finally the unforgiveable is ricocheting off the walls.

"Nobody would know." My father changed tack, in case maybe I knew what I was talking about.

"Oh, Dad, we can't do this." Would Nana have suggested this at a white cemetery? I wondered. I didn't think so.

"Why not? I can still climb."

"Daddy!" I whined the more intimate child-name, even as we were flying apart. Here we were, back in Darby, next to Collingdale, where I had worked in the five-and-ten and Ms. Agnes took uneaten hot dogs off people's plates and put them into the soup. Fifteen minutes ago Dad and I had stood on ground reserved to inter (and reinter) the bodies of African Americans with dignity. And here we were losing ours.

Dad stifled his own laugh.

I breathed deeply and pulled myself back into adulthood. Then I summoned Mozart's *Requiem in D minor* to distract me from the rage that was beginning to roll around at the bottom of my belly. Also Carole's voice telling me: "Girl, it's not that deep."

Right. Thanks. Phew.

Dad could see I'd mastered myself. Was he trying to goad me? "You know I've always been cheap." That made him chuckle some more.

"And you know that that's a subject where my sense of humor fails me."

Dad thought *that* was *very* funny. He laughed until he coughed.

"Okay, Dad, here: tell me so I can try to understand. What could be wrong with paying a historic black cemetery a reasonable fee for burial? There's a cement liner for the ashes, and they pay a guy to mow the lawn and dig the hole and close it back? Why shouldn't they get paid? I mean, we don't begrudge these Donut people two dollars for a cup of coffee that's not even very good."

"You don't like the coffee? I like the coffee."

My getting serious just seemed funnier and funnier to him.

"No. But you get my point. Why not pay these black people for their service?"

Dad told me a story about a burial he had watched as a preteen, when many of his stories came from, just about the time his parents separated, and he experienced a deep sadness that he turned inward. You'd have to have kept it to yourself with Nana, I'm sure. Was it depression? How can I tell? In any event, Dad saw the big casket and the even bigger cement liner and heard how much it all cost. From Nana's separation from Dad's father and on through his teen years, there was scarcity and bitterness about it that I know from having seen old letters and hearing them talk. Somehow this funeral got caught up in that impressionable and wounded period. Dad said that the whole funeral thing seemed like a scam to make fat cats fatter. Funerals trigger it for him. And everybody else just accepts it.

I told Dad that we were not burying an entire body, but a couple handfuls of ashes. Meaning that the liner would be small, and the cost minimal.

It was still a waste, he argued, and besides, his mother had asked him, specifically, to do this one thing for her. "Dying wish" figured in again.

Clouds hovered close, just to keep everything as gloomy as possible. We didn't need Dad's permission to bury Nana. Nor did I have to act as if I were taking seriously this crazy screed against burial grounds. Truth is, I had long ago stopped trying to speak truthfully to Dad, just as I stopped believing what he told me, whether it had to do with facts from the past or the reason he couldn't come pick up one of the children after school. Years of don't-ask-don't-tell had hollowed out the integrity of our relationship. I buried the love I still felt for him to protect what was left. I wished Carole were here, because she did not shut down as quickly as I did with him.

Wait a minute; that was it. I'd been arguing on his terms, instead of my own. "And what about Carole?" I asked.

"What do you mean?"

"You and I break into Eden, dispose of Nana, and what about Carole? What do you say to her? 'Sorry if you wanted closure with your family, but now it's, like, game over?'"

"Oh. I didn't think about that."

"Neither did Nana. But she should have."

Once Dad signed the papers and we found the Hagans plot, I drove him back to the house where I grew up. He still lived in the downstairs apartment. After renter nightmares, Dad and his girlfriend had given the second floor over to a couple of cats, who behaved much better. We stayed in the car for twenty more tense minutes. This trip had reminded Dad of going to find his own grandmother's grave, his father's mother's, she who left a hundred dollars for his college education with his father. His father, however, had refused to give him the money when he came for it at the start of his freshman year at Lincoln University. It was one of his signature anecdotes. I told Dad that I couldn't listen to that story one more time, because he had done something similar to me and never acknowledged it; never even saw the parallel. After my first term, he had failed to pay the modest tuition payment assessed him by the University of Pennsylvania. I'd been given scholarships and loans, yes, but the financial aid office's calculation was based on my having a working father able to contribute something. That amount had to be paid. After the first year, he didn't pay it.

"So I had to make up the difference myself. During my college career I worked between twenty and thirty, sometimes forty hours a week."

In 1974, when Dad had told me he couldn't pay the next tuition assessment, he instructed me to look up his old college friend who worked at Penn to help me find more money. That friend, I found out, was a librarian, and I remember being mortified when he kindly directed me to financial aid, where I had just been. I determined thereafter to make it through college without Dad's money and without asking him for help. God bless the child, I said. Who the hell needs more humiliation? And thanks, in large part to my boarding school preparation and a strong constitution, I was able to do it. It was very possible, however, despite complaining to friends about the hardship of full-time work and school, I had never told my father. "You didn't know that?"

"Not to that extent, no."

The rain had stopped. Having successfully overridden our usual patterns of speech, we felt more like people sharing grief than like people shielding themselves from each other.

"Why, Dad? All my life you guys talked about saving for our college."

Dad was squinting into his lap. "Your mother and I broke up . . . and . . . there were lawyers to pay . . ."

His face turned toward me with an expression I couldn't read, except that it was not apologetic. He had answered me without deflection. We had been honest. There was that, at least.

"Lawyers? Dad, geez."

Wintry sun tried to dry the streaky windshield as we both

stared straight ahead at the porch where I used to play. Numbers painted on the brick were the exact ones from fifty years before, faded but intact. Dad's girlfriend might come out the front door anytime to have a cigarette like my mom used to do. She'd wonder why we were sitting in the car in the cold.

"But eight years later, Dad, you did the same thing to Carole. The same thing. In college, she worked like a maniac. And let's face it, Dad, she was your special one." I thought of Carole as a preschooler, sitting at the top of the steps in her nightgown like a brown Cindy Lou Who, waiting for Dad to come home from hanging out for hours after judo practice. "How could you do it to her, too?"

Dad didn't argue, but it took him a while to turn toward me. He was shaking his head, incredulous. Then he asked, "Didn't my mother pay for her college?"

Nana? Why would he think Nana paid? We were back to Crazy Land. How could we have lived all these years in close proximity, everyone seeing each other: Sunday afternoon dinners and Christmases and trips to the zoo and the Franklin Museum and the ACME and the Academy of Natural Sciences and baptisms and doctors' appointments? And Dad: how could he have sat in the office with Nana every Monday, Tuesday, Thursday, and Friday morning for years after he retired, God help him, at fifty-five, and assumed, but never asked?

But maybe we'd left the truth behind. Did he really believe Nana had paid Carole's tuition or was he making an excuse? Was this a delusion? Could it have been a misunderstanding connected to what I'd come to think of as the brittle remnant of Hagans pride, just the pride, minus land and money, minus Napoleon Hagans's accomplishment or Will Hagans's ambition, without anything but a pointless competitiveness that could make us chew each other alive, like Jack Russells left alone in the barn? It felt like that pride had to be at the heart of the thoughtless, selfish dig-a-hole command of Nana's, and Dad's willingness to do it, as if regular rules didn't apply to him. I had hated that pride and hated it now.

But had I substituted my own? My father's face, almost on the edge of disgust, made me think that maybe I'd taken the brittleness wrong. Maybe stealing a hole in the ground was a mark of shame. If we used the American ideal of each generation building on the achievements of the last, then we had not lived up to Napoleon Hagans's legacy. We hadn't gotten bigger and wealthier and more powerful in each generation. Will Hagans had hitched his career to the black man who got into Congress from North Carolina, but Jim Crow laws and lynchings made sure that every gain would be paid for in blood and money, if not by them, then by other black people, somewhere. How could Nana know this when she didn't even know her father's stories, only his Anglophilia and Christmas hunting parties on Napoleon's land, and the good cigars and elbows off the table?

Did Nana know how, as president of the black Citizens Republican Club of Philadelphia, his job was to help his tribe "grow rich not by labor, but by the credit and capital they command" in order to slip the noose of white capital; that he'd been a member of the Pen and Pencil Club in Washington with the sons of Frederick Douglass, and editors of *The Washington Bee* and *The Colored American*, writing in the early 1900s that black lives mattered even as the new NAACP hoisted above Fifth Avenue in New York the dread flag: A MAN WAS LYNCHED YESTERDAY; that as the South snatched back the vote from blacks in the South, he tried the North, which was so over Negroes, and where he lost his wife, and then, in the Depression, his own capital?

Did she understand how thoroughly and strategically America had worked to stop black people from holding onto wealth, just as federal and local redlining kept us from gaining the financial foothold of freely selected real estate? I don't think so. Like America itself, she suspected that it was our fault that we failed to clear the hurdles, our inferiority that kept us from Race-Mission Impossible. Nana wanted her descendants' accomplishments to match those of her predecessors and prove America wrong. But our small clan had not stayed married, or advanced in government, business, or the arts. Nana would go into the same National Register of Historic Places cemetery with her father and mother, not in peace, but restlessly, poured into the ground as if from an ashtray by descendants sneaking in like thieves.

"No, Dad, Nana didn't pay for Carole's education."

My heart pounded again, as if I were feeling everything he hadn't or couldn't, but should have. The car was getting very cold.

"You want to come in for a little while?"

"No, Dad. I'll go home now."

ᴄᴖ

Nana's early December funeral—service performed by Bob in church, concrete liner provided by the cemetery, ashes deposited publicly with mourners gathered together in the daytime—began a Christmas season for me that was both muted and simple. Carole and Karline cleared Nana's bedsit—where she had no doubt worked my father over about the hole-and-shovel routine—and returned it to a family room. It felt like Maundy Thursday, when the altar is stripped bare and we sing the Bach *Passion Chorale*: "My days are few, O fail not, with thine immortal power, / To hold me that I quail not in death's most fearful hour."

I had been quailing something awful, and it wasn't I who was dying.

I thought I should feel free, but I didn't. Caretaking chores dropped away, but a fine-milled rage dusted the corners of my grief like the powdery mildew that used to attack Nana's tea roses. It sent out spores: I was nervous. I kept thinking I'd forgotten something. Yet, even the dog stopped guarding where Nana had slept, and came back to lie at the foot of our bed.

At Art Sanctuary, the tenth-anniversary events had finished in triumph and, as if I were competent to take on new work, I accepted a new project, thinking it would be good for me. I was to write scripts for video narratives about the enslaved people in President Washington's executive mansion in Philadelphia, now part of Independence Park, next to the Liberty Bell. But I had no idea what I was getting into. My first meeting was two days after the funeral. The group that had recruited me and filmmaker Louis Massiah as their new black creative team had been at this project for two years. Architects, historians, representatives of politicians and the tourism industry, National Park Service experts, activists of several stripes: they sat poised around a square made from many tables, end to end. When our historians presented their complicated vision for the President's House, an open-air house museum next to the Liberty Bell, and it failed to put President Washington's enslaved Africans at the center of interpretation, the meeting devolved from a community scrum into a verbal brawl. Had I seen the conflict ahead, within the creative team and the community watch group, I would have been even more jacked up as I learned the sickening legal minutiae founders agreed on to make slavery work as they created our free country.

Then, throughout December, Lessons and Carols, the Christmas pageant, the Christmas Eve service—they poured themselves into a great Advent Vitamix. I sputtered and choked on the big red-and-green smoothie like a driver who can't find a rest area.

By January I was full-up with exhaustion. Bob took me to Puerto Rico for a few days, and when we sat in the sun I wished I could turn myself inside out to dry. The grief needed more light and air than I could take in.

As winter let go, I finally felt I had the wherewithal to take my nephews for the weekend. We drove back from Montclair, New Jersey, in our minivan. They loved to scramble all the way back to the third row and shout forward to me in the driver's seat. This trip was the death-theme drive:

"How did Nana die?"

"Were you there?"

"What did she look like?"

"Did it hurt?"

"Is she back in her old house now?"

Funny, intuitive question, that.

After I returned to Philadelphia, Nana came to me in dreams. She was sitting in her wheelchair, banging her fists on the padded arms, demanding that I get her back into her house in New Jersey. Weak and clouded over with cataracts she'd refused to have removed, her eyes nevertheless burned into me. "Get me into my house," she shouted. "I want to come back."

We'd have to clear the house, give away the storage locker full of tchotchkes, and sell it four years into the recession in order to honor the named gifts of money in Nana's will; I could only hope there would be enough to cover them all.

But the dream was not about practical facts. It was about my fury and hers, which seemed to have escaped the dream. A haunting was beginning, and I had to stop it. I'd thought this was a dream, but now my eyes were open, and although Bob's quiet, even breath was beside me, I heard in it the death rattle. When I closed my eyes, she was there, in the wheelchair, frowning, impatient, demanding an answer.

Ten years later, I wrote to clear away the rage, uncover the simple grief, stored in the muscles that seized up then and cannot remember how they were before, and to convince us both, Nana and myself, that she has left this plane. And to forgive.

It has taken some doing.

Turns out you can't just threaten. Like Nana couldn't just die. Like we couldn't just sell her house. Like I couldn't just renovate the Dickerson Building. Like I couldn't find a way out of the bitterness of finding that her love wasn't what I'd thought. Nor was mine.

Turns out I was to write the libretto for a mini-opera with composer Liliya Ugay. I wrote a mezzo-soprano part for the character of Nana's Ghost, who wants to find the libretto about her haunting and destroy it. She knows that when it is performed, she will really have to die and leave Granddaughter alone. But it turns out that, after writing the damned thing, the granddaughter is not sure she wants that either:

Granddaughter: *It felt like I was losing you.*
Nana's Ghost: *You are. Love would mean that I should go.*

Granddaughter hands Nana's Ghost the portfolio bag she's been looking for, but Nana's Ghost does not take it. *Where I'm going,* she sings, *what would I do with paper? Or a bell?*

The line that I wrote and deleted, ten or fifteen times, never made it into the final version: *You never hit me when I was small.* It didn't sing on its own, and it would have pushed the music into drama that would have competed with the final resolution. This was a thirty-minute piece, max. But I'd needed that line for myself, to open the box I'd kept locked as tightly as Nana kept hers.

I didn't realize, consciously, that I would finish this book about Nana on Ash Wednesday, the beginning of the Lenten season of reflection that precedes the ritual remembrance of Jesus's last ministries, crucifixion, and the empty tomb. But I did and I am. It's two years after a late-life yoga practice let my body begin to feel Nana's loss, and the first writing I did linked her death to my life. That was on Ash Wednesday, too. My young yoga teacher sat down next to me and said, "I think you can do this pose today." It would be my first try at Marichyasana D, or Marichi's Pose for short.

Meghan's hair is naturally the auburn color Nana dyed hers in her last fifty years. Meghan pays her students exquisite and generous, but not fussy, attention. The pose starts with left leg in half lotus. I bend the right knee, plant my heel in front of the hip, and let my body tip forward. Then there's twisting the torso to allow the left shoulder to lie on the outside of the bent knee, and the left arm to wrap around the right leg and through space back toward the left rib cage. The other arm reaches around the back to catch, or as yogis say, bind, it. Oh boy.

Meghan smiled, with humor and compassion. "Now breathe," she said.

But since that was clearly impossible, the voices began their suffocating comedy routine: *Breathe? Where? How? What's the point? Just wait out the five supposed "breath" count! Hold your breath! They don't call it a bind for nothing! How can a bind free the spirit?*

"You have to breathe." Meghan can be insistent.

Nah, baby. Not me. I did asthma in second grade with Mrs. Zuckerman. I did the Philadelphia School Reform Commission till midnight with no effing inhaler. Almost drowned at fourteen. You may have to breathe. Me? I can fake it.

"Breathe into here." Meghan cupped the area in the upper back that was most compressed.

It's a deep, brick well with pain at the bottom. I throw things into it like colonial-era people threw broken crockery and rusty straightening combs into their wells. It has hurt for years and seized up completely that first winter Nana came to live with us in the rectory. Usually, despite its being omni-present, I don't feel it. Still, it's where the lynching scene came from in my last book. It's where my video of slavery runs and runs and runs. Who could breathe into that? How do you sing Rusalka in a straitjacket? Or Mahalia?

"We breathe into the places where it feels most constricted."

Damned if the fool puppy-dog internal spirit doesn't try. And then some air, something, some that-ness happens where there was nothing before but constriction. My torso turns, and the hands bind, as if controlled not by me, but by this breathing that comes into me as a triumph of discipline over good sense.

"Wow," Meghan said, getting up to help someone else. "That's great. Do five breaths there. That's what we do in yoga. We make space in the body."

Comedy routine again: Milton Berle and Kevin Hart, together at last, in drag, talking over each other. *Oh, we do, do we? Space in the body. Remember pregnancies? Now that was making space! But what're we working with today: one heart, two lungs, one stomach, spleen, guts . . . and, sweetheart, hate to mention it, but, like thirty extra pounds. So, let's face it, Boo, you're lucky to get this far. And, by the way, what are WE making space for, anyway?*

Shhh. Shhh. Shhh.

Hips and shoulders rotated in opposite directions, a taste of flight, on earth as it is in heaven. I hear a sound like Nana's last breaths as Zoë and I sat, holding her cold hands. My own breath is dry and angry, afraid, to be sure, but it is not my last. A few years ago, I breathed past an illusion of exhaling through the wall of the stomach something hard and black, as if I'd breathed it in from her rattling exhale. I am still breathing freely. I will still enjoy hot tea and warm muscles; I will hold my husband at night; I will meet new grandchildren and let new love pour through this tired body resurrected after almost giving up more than once.

And then I hear it, what I listen for when I write, and when I pray: neither sound nor vision, only perfect communication, a slow answering life breath: "You make space in the body for God."

Acknowledgments

I am grateful to acknowledge the generous contributions of people whose extraordinary care—for Nana, for my family and me, and for this book—made *Ladysitting* possible.

On behalf of Nana: thanks to Roosevelt Cochran, Michael Horsey, Yolanda McBride, Roman McDonald, and Sean Davis. I am personally indebted, as is our entire family, to Gertrude Dunlap, Karline Venord, Craig Alston, and Mike Wogan for their attention to Nana and her needs and ours.

For their work to document the lives of free North Carolina people of color, including the Haganses: many thanks to newly discovered cousin Lisa Y. Henderson and family genealogists Bill Hagans, now deceased, and Wanda Mercer.

For encouragement, played as if it were an extreme sport: love and gratitude to Tina Smith-Brown, Sasha Anawalt, Dana Ridley, Hannibal Lokumbe, Rebecca Alpert, Helen Cunningham, and Ted Newbold.

For allowing me to read from early versions of the book and discover what was possible: thanks to the 2016 Festival of Faith and Writing; and special thanks to Ethel Rackin and the Wordsmith Reading Series of Bucks County Community College.

For mind/body healing and discovery: thank you, Dr. Wilfreda Baugh, Melissa Cotton, Carol Huth, Meghan Kirk, Angela Moore-Colley and Herb Colley, Dr. Martin Mulders, Dr. Nancy Post, Julia Taylor, John Vitarelli..

For trust and guidance: thanks to my agent Jane Dystel; and for finding what was missing that I couldn't see: thanks to my editor Amy Cherry.

For living in abundance as we bring our generations forward: love and gratitude to Carole and Michael, Joshua and Coleman.

For generosity of heart that few mothers are blessed to receive, and for sharp minds, unleashed when necessary: love and appreciation to Laura and Zoë.

For the full-catastrophe life and one pastoral edit after another: love to Bob, more than we can ask or imagine.

LADYSITTING

Lorene Cary

LADYSITTING

Lorene Cary

DISCUSSION QUESTIONS

1. What does Cary mean when she says she and her siblings were "brought up by hand" (p. 9)? Why was this important? How were Cary's weekends with Nana different?

2. Before Cary marries, she tells her white husband-to-be that "being black . . . mattered urgently" to her, and that her family "had lots of shades and varieties of black experience to live with" (p. 26). In what ways does Cary's marriage contribute to her family's racial heritage?

3. Years before, when Cary divorced her first husband, she felt she had followed the family's generations-long pattern of divorce. How does this common thread affect her adult relationship with Nana?

4. Cary's great-great grandfather was a successful, but illiterate, landowner who raised cotton on some land and rented out the rest. His well-educated sons became politically active "race men," each serving as secretary to Congressman George Henry White, the last African American to serve from North Carolina in more than ninety years. Why was it important to include their stories and Reconstruction-era politics in a book about caretaking in contemporary America?

5. On page 48, this is how Cary describes the South from which Nana's father would soon move his family: " . . . in a sustained campaign that historian Jan Carew calls 'total war,' the Jim Crow Democrats and their supporters clawed back control, using laws, voter suppression, books and songs depicting black inferiority, and a campaign of terror." How does the history of America's cultural depiction of black inferiority affect Cary's book-length consideration of her own family's pride and shame?

6. Cary finds stashes of cash in Nana's home because Nana distrusts banks to keep her money safe. Is being African American a factor? Or the depression? Or Pop-Pop's end-of-life finances? How did Nana think of race and money?

7. In Chapter 4, Cary recalls times with other relatives and in-laws at the ends of their lives. What do those people's lives and deaths have to do with Nana? How does Cary's experience of death and dying deepen over time?

8. How does Nana's selling the last of her rental properties affect her fierce sense of independence?

9. Cary tells and then retells Nana's childhood story of her mother sending her into the field to collect cotton for her first doll. Why does Cary come back to the story and challenge it? What is this memoir saying about memory itself?

10. Later Cary starts, forgets, and then revisits with Nana a folktale Nana used to read to her and that they referred to as Cary grew up. What is it that makes this the one story, out of many others, that she tells and that Nana enjoys?

11. Nana often seems cool toward religious practice, but enjoys many benefits of living in a religious community. What is her relationship to the parish of Good Shepherd and its activities? How does the text, with its many references to Christianity, speak of spirituality more generally?

12. *Ladysitting* is very much about intergenerational relationships. How does caring for Nana influence Zoë? How does their relationship evolve during that time? Older sister Laura does not live at home; what is her involvement in the family's ladysitting, and how does it affect her young adult life?

13. As Nana's time grows short, she becomes paranoid about those around her, eventually turning on Cary. What does she mean when she talks about "the fix I'm in" (p. 207)?

14. When Cary's sister and her family come to visit, Cary quotes her sister's "signature laugh line, 'Why are we like this? What did they do to us?'" (p. 214). Which shared qualities is she referring to? What answers does *Ladysitting* suggest?

15. On pages 217, Nana asks if Cary "[wants her] dead." Before she answers, the chapter stops time to give an extended meditation on what Cary was feeling and thinking. What do we learn in those two pages about the experience of caretaking?

16. Cary and her daughter feel "stunned" when Nana dies (p. 236). In what ways does this illustrate the deep meaning and emotion in caring for Nana at the end of her life? Why do you think Cary didn't write *Ladysitting* until ten years after Nana's death?

Diana Abu-Jaber	*Life Without a Recipe*
Diane Ackerman	*The Zookeeper's Wife*
Michelle Adelman	*Piece of Mind*
Molly Antopol	*The UnAmericans*
Andrea Barrett	*Archangel*
Rowan Hisayo Buchanan	*Harmless Like You**
Ada Calhoun	*Wedding Toasts I'll Never Give**
Bonnie Jo Campbell	*Mothers, Tell Your Daughters*
	Once Upon a River
Lan Samantha Chang	*Inheritance*
Ann Cherian	*A Good Indian Wife*
Evgenia Citkowitz	*The Shades**
Amanda Coe	*The Love She Left Behind*
Michael Cox	*The Meaning of Night*
Jeremy Dauber	*Jewish Comedy**
Jared Diamond	*Guns, Germs, and Steel*
Caitlin Doughty	*From Here to Eternity**
Andre Dubus III	*House of Sand and Fog*
	Townie: A Memoir
Anne Enright	*The Forgotten Waltz*
	The Green Road
Amanda Filipacchi	*The Unfortunate Importance of Beauty*
Beth Ann Fennelly	*Heating & Cooling**
Betty Friedan	*The Feminine Mystique**
Maureen Gibbon	*Paris Red*
Stephen Greenblatt	*The Swerve**
Lawrence Hill	*The Illegal*
	Someone Knows My Name
Ann Hood	*The Book That Matters Most*
	The Obituary Writer
Dara Horn	*A Guide for the Perplexed*
Blair Hurley	*The Devoted**

Meghan Kenny	*The Driest Season**
Nicole Krauss	*The History of Love*
Don Lee	*The Collective**
Amy Liptrot	*The Outrun: A Memoir*
Donna M. Lucey	*Sargent's Women**
Bernard MacLaverty	*Midwinter Break**
Maaza Mengiste	*Beneath the Lion's Gaze*
Claire Messud	*The Burning Girl*
	When the World Was Steady
Liz Moore	*Heft*
	The Unseen World
Neel Mukherjee	*The Lives of Others*
	*A State of Freedom**
Janice P. Nimura	*Daughters of the Samurai**
Rachel Pearson	*No Apparent Distress**
Richard Powers	*Orfeo*
Kirstin Valdez Quade	*Night at the Fiestas*
Jean Rhys	*Wide Sargasso Sea*
Mary Roach	*Packing for Mars**
Somini Sengupta	*The End of Karma**
Akhil Sharma	*Family Life*
	*A Life of Adventure and Delight**
Joan Silber	*Fools**
Johanna Skibsrud	*Quartet for the End of Time*
Mark Slouka	*Brewster*
Kate Southwood	*Evensong*
Manil Suri	*The City of Devi*
	The Age of Shiva
Madeleine Thien	*Do Not Say We Have Nothing*
	Dogs at the Perimeter
Vu Tran	*Dragonfish*
Rose Tremain	*The American Lover*
	The Gustav Sonata
Brady Udall	*The Lonely Polygamist*
Brad Watson	*Miss Jane*
Constance Fenimore Woolson	*Miss Grief and Other Stories**

*Available only on the Norton website